DIALECTICAL BEHAVIOR THERAPY

Children

&

Adolescents

CONNIE CALLAHAN, PH.D., LPCC, LMFT

PESI®

EAU CLAIRE, WISCONSIN

PESI, LLC
PO Box 1000
3839 White Avenue
Eau Claire, Wisconsin 54702

Printed in the United States of America

ISBN: 978-0-9790218-9-3

PESI, LLC strives to obtain knowledgeable authors and faculty for its publications and seminars. The clinical recommendations contained herein are the result of extensive author research and review. Obviously, any recommendations for patient care must be held up against individual circumstances at hand. To the best of our knowledge any recommendations included by the author or faculty reflect currently accepted practice. However, these recommendations cannot be considered universal and complete. The authors and publisher repudiate any responsibility for unfavorable effects that result from information, recommendations, undetected omissions or errors. Professionals using this publication should research other original sources of authority as well.

For information on this and other PESI manuals and
audio recordings, please call 800-844-8260 or
visit our website at www.pesi.com

ABOUT THE AUTHOR

Connie Callahan, Ph.D., LPCC, LMFT, is the Chair of the Counseling and Educational Psychology Department at Eastern Kentucky University. She has practiced as a Licensed Professional Clinical Counselor and a Licensed Marriage and Family Therapist since 1986 in a variety of settings. Dr. Callahan has been using researched based interventions with clients, supervisees, and colleagues in various treatment settings and graduate programs for over two decades, and is known nationally as an expert trainer, clinical supervisor, clinician and acclaimed PESI presenter.

Dr. Callahan has worked with dozens of clinicians and organizations to integrate researched based interventions in clinical practices and program models. She has over 30 years in mental health treatment settings across all levels of care. Dr. Callahan provides licensure supervision and collegial consultation to mental health, school and dual diagnosis clinicians. She also works with systems of care and individual clinicians to implement and sustain evidenced based practices with a variety of mental disorders. She publishes regularly in journals and books.

TABLE OF CONTENTS

Dialectal behavior therapy (DBT) was devised by Marsha Linehan (1993a) to treat persons diagnosed with borderline personality disorder (BPD). This book was titled *Cognitive-Behavioral Treatment of Borderline Personality Disorder.* Linehan first worked with clients who were chronically suicidal and women who met criteria for borderline personality disorder. These clients posed significant challenges as many of them required therapy for multiple and complex Axis I problems (Goldfried & Davison, 1976). Linehan at first used clinical behavior therapy with her clients but the nature of her clients' problems encouraged her to balance and complement behavior therapy with other therapeutic strategies. Her careful research into the efficacy of her treatment approach led her to develop treatment manuals (Linehan, 1993a, 1993b). These manuals organize treatment strategies into protocols and structured treatment and clinical decision making so that therapists can respond flexibly to meet client needs. Linehan's DBT is a comprehensive approach to treating this disorder and may be applied to other clinical problems.

Clients with borderline personality disorder are normally adults who present with a variety of symptoms which keep them from functioning well in life. Many of those symptoms began in childhood for a variety of reasons and culminated in severe problems for those trying to live adult lives. Our supposition is that since these problems began in childhood, a proper place to begin working on the problems is when they begin to develop.

DBT utilizes empirically supported behavior therapy protocols to treat Axis I problems. These include interventions in behavior therapy that are common to all behavior therapies (e.g. cognitive behavior therapy, cognitive restructuring, exposure and response prevention, skills training including stimulus control, reinforcement, therapist reciprocal vulnerability, and irreverence). DBT also features interventions unique to dialectical behavior therapy like targeting: primary (e.g., suicidal, therapy interfering behaviors) and secondary (e.g., inhibited grieving), mindfulness as a set of skills, dialectical focus, emotion regulation and opposite action skills, distress tolerance skills, high degree of therapist self-disclosure, microanalytic chain analysis, commitment strategies, validation as an explicit therapist skill set and telephone consultation.

DBT therapy involves therapists working as individual psychotherapists with clients while at the same time helping clients learn new skills by being involved in group skills training. To ensure that clients begin to apply skills they learn in groups, the DBT therapists coach their clients through telephone consultation. To adhere to the principles of DBT, the individual psychotherapist becomes part of a DBT treatment team. Clients are normally in therapy for the period of one year.

DBT follows a format with regard to group skills training. DBT recognizes that individuals with Borderline Personality Disorder often end up with crises and problems in their lives because they lack skills to help them cope with life in a positive manner. For that reason, DBT embraces a broad curriculum of skills training with 23 sets of skills that are taught. The training format consists of a year-long program with weekly 2- to 2.5-hour classes of about 8 patients and 2 facilitators. The facilitators work in the skills training groups and they also may function as individual therapists for the group members.

This poses an interesting reality for practitioners who work with children and teenagers. Individual psychotherapy may rely heavily on cognitive interventions while the skills training consists of 23 skill sets. Often, practitioners may not be in a setting where they can carry out 23 skills training sessions with clients and keep them in therapy for at least a year. Sometimes parents bring in youths only when there is a crisis and after the crisis abates, the parents quit bringing the young persons to therapy. Sometimes the number of sessions with clients are limited by managed care protocols. Therapists may need to assess client problems and provide treatment strategies that will assist young people with limitations to therapy. Providing tools to help young people cope with life can be done with DBT even with those limitations. While it is much more efficacious to provide therapy using Linehan's full DBT model, clinicians may be forced to choose interventions that work with young people.

In DBT practice, clinicians organize therapy into stages and targets (Linehan, 1996) and, with very few exceptions, adhere strictly to the order in which problems are addressed. The organization into stages and targets prevents DBT being a service that, week after week, addresses the crisis of the moment. Further, it has a logical progression that:

- first addresses behaviors that could lead to the client's death,
- then behaviors that could lead to premature termination,
- to behaviors that destroy the quality of life,
- to the need for alternative skills.

Chapter 2 will provide readers with specifics for working with self-harming behaviors. For addressing behaviors that might lead to premature termination, Marsha Linehan (1995) provides an excellent video example of handling this issue in her video

CD, *Treating Borderline Personality Disorder: The Dialectical Approach*. In her film, Linehan informed her client that she intended to examine any behaviors that might interfere with therapy. She very clearly stated to her client, "If you do anything that interferes with therapy, I will bring this up and if I do anything that interferes with therapy, you bring it up." A clinician would then deal with issues that might arise.

The rest of the chapters provide interventions that help youths understand behaviors that destroy the quality of life and the need for alternative skills.

This treatment manual seeks to address behaviors that could lead to the client's death, behaviors that destroy quality of life, and alternative skills in the form of interventions that help young clients with emotional regulation. This manual seeks to provide clinicians with interventions that address client deficits in behavioral capabilities needed to make life changes.

SELF-HARMING BEHAVIORS: SUICIDE AND SELF-MUTILATING

One of the first processes a clinician would follow would be to have a very frank discussion with the client about any suicidal gestures, attempts, or self-mutilating behaviors. Next, the clinician would assess behaviors that destroy the quality of life of the child or teenager. While many behaviors may destroy quality of life, one of the most disturbing behaviors is self-mutilation. The other is suicidal behavioral including suicidal ideation and suicidal gestures.

Self-mutilation is intentional self destructive behavior that destroys body tissue. This occurs in 24–40% of psychiatric patients and 750 out of 100,000 of the general population. It is not the same psychological process as suicidal ideation. In self-mutilation, self-inflicted wounds are repeated, superficial and numerous. They occur in a short time span and are normally done with conscious awareness of the consequences of the behavior. Self-mutilation is a complex group of behaviors including deliberate destruction or alteration of body tissue without conscious suicidal intent. It is deliberate, non-life threatening, self-effected bodily harm or disfigurement of a socially unacceptable nature.

People who self-mutilate often have a history of being neglected as well as sexually and physically abused as children. This behavior is used when the affective state is too intense for the individual; there is often numbing and anger. Adolescents who self-mutilate are often overwhelmed with feelings, feel alone, even if part of a group, involve both girls and boys, and may be at times learned from a friendship group. A history of abuse may or may not be present. In youths, common patterns of self-mutilating behavior may include:

- Cutting
- Erasing (Using rubber or cement to cause an abrasion)
- Picking
- Picking at scabs or surgical wound

Individuals self-mutilate when they are angry, lonely, scared and fearful of abandonment.

This is different than suicidal behavior. **Parasuicidal behaviors** are those actions that are intentionally self injurious, such as cutting the wrists or taking a non-lethal overdose of drugs. **Suicidal ideation** refers to a person's thoughts about suicide. This means a person is thinking about suicide but has no plan. This is not uncommon.

About 3–4% of adolescents will have considered suicide in the last two weeks.

However, these thoughts are much more likely, and more likely to be serious, if a client has previously made a suicide attempt, is depressed, or is pessimistic. Clients who are still depressed and have made previous suicide attempts are extremely likely to be thinking seriously about suicide.

Completed suicide refers to willful, self-inflicted, life threatening acts that result in death. **Level of lethality** refers to the seriousness of a suicide threat– the degree to which it is likely to result in death. The National Center for Health Statistics ranked suicide as the eleventh cause of death in the US. One person every 16.6 minutes completes a suicide. Teenagers and preteens have a high risk factor; suicide is the third cause of death

In working with adolescents, there are three characteristics that clinicians must consider: adolescent egocentrism, the imaginary audience, and the personal fable. With adolescent egocentrism, clinicians must realize that many adolescents have a tendency to define the world only as it applies to them. They become preoccupied with their own thought process. They view the world only in terms of: *How does this affect me?* With the imaginary audience, teens may become preoccupied with their own thinking and self-consciousness about physical and sexual changes. They often create an imaginary audience and believe that they are continually under observation by others. They anticipate the reactions of others as if others see them as they see themselves. They think that others are as intensely interested in the minute details of their appearance and behavior as they are.

With the personal fable, teens fail to separate their concerns from those of others. They over differentiate their own feelings and see themselves as new and different than anyone else. Therefore, they regard themselves as special and unique—a one-of-a-kind individual whom no one else can quite understand. This can lead to the feeling that they are immune form the bad things that happen in life or that nothing will ever really happen to them.

These characteristics are important to understand. Clinicians should not dismiss them. Adults realize that most people are too involved in themselves to be watching others that closely. Adults know that bad things do happen and that others can learn to cope. Therapists understand that we don't always get what we want in life and often we have to work hard to make life work. Life just isn't about us. However, young people don't know those things. As clinicians listen to others, they must truly enter others' phenomenological worlds.

Suicide attempts mean persons have actually tried to hurt themselves. These can be medically serious or not serious. They can be psychologically serious or not. About

40% of teenagers will have thought about suicide for only a half hour or so before they try something. The most frequent reason for these impulsive suicide plans are relationship problems. Some facts to remember: There are three female attempts for every male attempt—females use pills or poison. Men use more legal means (guns, hanging) and 4.1 men die for each female who completes suicide.

Suicidal behavior is often an outcome of untreated depression. Risk increases with use of alcohol or other substances. Three ingredients for higher risk for suicide completion include social isolation, hopelessness, and inability to problem solve. Adolescents with psychotic depression have a high risk for completing suicide. This is due to the following:

- Depression
- Social withdrawal
- Guilt
- Paranoid thoughts
- Delusions
- Hopelessness
- Worthlessness

Assessment and therapeutic work for self harm is briefly discussed in Chapter 2.

LINEHAN'S (1999) BEHAVIORAL PATTERNS IN BORDERLINE PERSONALITY DISORDER (BPD)

Besides staging as an important approach to therapy, dealing with problems areas in youths' lives is important. Marsha Linehan with Dialectical Behavior Therapy suggested that there are six difficult problems clients face:

1. *Emotional vulnerability*
2. *Self-invalidation*
3. *Unrelenting crises*
4. *Active passivity*
5. *Inhibited grieving*
6. *Apparent competence*

Emotional vulnerability is a pattern of pervasive difficulties in regulating negative emotions, including:

- high sensitivity to negative emotional stimuli,
- high emotion intensity, and
- slow return to emotional baseline, as well as awareness and experience of emotional vulnerability.

This may include a tendency to blame the social environment for unrealistic expectations and demands.

Self-invalidation is the tendency to invalidate or fail to recognize one's own emotion responses, thoughts, beliefs, and behaviors. The self-invalidating client usually will set unrealistically high standards and expectations for himself or herself. This may include intense shame, self-hate, and self-directed anger. Often this problem stems from invalidating environments.

An invalidating environment is one in which communication of private experiences is met by erratic, inappropriate, and extreme responses. In other words, the expression of private experiences is not validated; instead, it is often punished, and/or trivialized. The experience of painful emotions, as well as the factors that to the emotional person seem causally related to the emotional distress, are disregarded. The individual's interpretations of her own behavior, including the experience of the intents and motivations associated with behavior, are dismissed (Linehan, 1993, p.49).

Unrelenting crises involve patterns of frequent, stressful, negative environmental events, disruptions, and roadblocks— some caused by the individual's dysfunctional lifestyle others by an inadequate social milieu, and many by fate or chance.

Active passivity is defined as the tendency to passive interpersonal problem-solving style, involving failure to engage actively in solving of own life problems, often together with active attempts to solicit problem solving from others in the environment and as a result of learned helplessness and hopelessness.

Inhibited grieving is the tendency to inhibit and over control negative emotional responses, especially those associated with grief and loss, including sadness, anger, guilt, shame, anxiety, and panic.

Apparent competence is the tendency for the individual to appear deceptively more competent than she actually is; usually due to failure of competencies to generalize across expected moods, situations, and time, and failure to display adequate nonverbal cues of emotional distress.

SIX AREAS OF ASSESSMENT

With each area of assessment, a clinician must ask, "Where is the child's most pressing need? What is causing the teen the most problem?" Then ask how many sessions there might actually be with a child and choose interventions that will help with the most pressing area of need and that match the number of actual sessions one may have with the young person.

Dealing with Self-Harm

ASSESSMENT

The purpose of assessment and screening is to obtain a comprehensive assessment to predict the client's self-destructive behavior, and to determine appropriate interventions.

Physical Domain

- Does the individual feel numb?
- Does the person distort how they experience his/her body sensations?
- Has the individual ever been abused?
  - Physically
  - Sexually
  - Raped
- Signs and symptoms of a physical illness
- Somatic complaints
- Neurovegetative signs: Difficulty concentrating, changes in appetite, decrease in energy, decrease in libido, changes in sleep pattern

Emotional Domain

- Any expressions of suicidal thoughts and/or feelings?

Assess antecedents of previous suicide attempt(s).

- When did you begin to have suicidal thoughts?
- Did any event (stressor) precipitate the suicidal thoughts?

Assess Personal Coping

- Tell me about your relationships with friends and family.
- Do you prefer being alone or being with friends?
- Do you have a close friend or relative with whom you shared your thoughts and feelings?
- How do you behave when you were sad? Angry? Happy?
- Tell me how school or your job is going.

Emotional Assessment

- Depressed mood; expressing no hope for the future
- Has the individual told anyone about his/her suicidal thoughts or plans?
- How does the person identify his/her self esteem and sense of accomplishment?
- Is the individual experiencing an intense emotional reaction, such as anger?
- Is the emotion similar to what was experienced during an abuse?
- Does the individual distort his/her feelings?
- If there have been previous attempts, you must also assess them.

To Assess Previous Attempts

1. How did the client try to kill himself or herself?
   - What method was used?

2. How serious was the action taken?
   - If the client overdosed, what pills were taken? How Many?
   - If the client cut, what body area was cut? Did the cuts require stitches?

3. To what degree did the client intend to die?
   - Did the client tell anyone about the attempt afterward or hint to anyone beforehand?
   - Was the attempt in an isolated area or where the client would be easily discovered?
   - Did the client write a will or a goodbye note?
   - How does the client feel about the fact that the attempt was NOT successful?
   - A good question to ask, "What are some of your thoughts about the fact that you are still alive?"

5. How well planned was this attempt, as opposed to an impulsive act?

6. Did alcohol or drugs play a role in the attempt?

7. Did interpersonal factors have a major role in the attempt?

   • Were there feelings of failure? ("People would be better off without me")
   • Was there anger toward people?
   • Some suicide attempts are undertaken to make others feel guilt.

8. Did a specific stressor or set of stressors prompt the attempt?

9. At the time of the attempt, how hopeless did the client feel?

10. Why did the attempt fail?

    • How was the client found, and how was help summoned?

Determine Present State of Mind

   • How often do you think about suicide? Do you feel as if you're a burden? Or that life isn't worth living?
   • What makes you feel better (e.g., contact with family, use of substances)?
   • What makes you feel worse (e.g., being alone)?
   • Do you have a plan to end your life?
   • How much control of your suicidal ideas do you have? Can you suppress them or call someone for help?
   • What stops you from killing yourself (e.g., family, religious beliefs)?

Cognitive Domain

   • Does the individual have thoughts that repeat, that are emotional and increase the drive to self-mutilate?
   • What are these thoughts?
   • When do the repeating thoughts occur?
   • What type of redirection is helpful, example, music with a driving beat
   • Has the person developed a suicide plan?
   • Is there a preoccupation with self?
   • Is judgment clouded with suicide as the only option?
   • Does the individual have insight into his/her problems or behavior?

Delineate the Extent of Ideation

   • When did you begin to have suicidal thoughts?
   • Did any event (stressor) precipitate the suicidal thoughts?
   • How often do you think about suicide? Do you feel as if you're a burden? Or that life isn't worth living?
   • What makes you feel better (e.g., contact with family, use of substances)?

- What makes you feel worse (e.g., being alone)?
- Do you have a plan to end your life?
- How much control of your suicidal ideas do you have? Can you suppress them or call someone for help?
- What stops you from killing yourself (e.g., family, religious beliefs)?

The Plan

- Does the client have a plan?
- You must determine how specific a suicidal plan is.
- When does s/he intend to kill himself/herself?
- Does the child have the means?
- The more specific the plan, the more danger there is.

Specificity

- Level of lethality
- Explicit thoughts of suicide,
- A weapon or plan chosen and available,
- History of a previous suicidal attempt,
- Perceives no support system,
- Has written a suicidal note and is unable to control the impulse

Ascertain Further Plans

- Do you own a gun or have access to firearms?
- Do you have access to potentially harmful medications?
- Have you imagined your funeral and how people will react to your death?
- Have you "practiced" your suicide? (e.g., put the gun to your head or held the medications in your hand)?

More Cognitive Assessment

- Does the individual have commanding hallucinations that are suicidal and/or homicidal?
- Is there a focus on negative themes, to the exclusion of other thoughts?

Command Hallucinations

- Command hallucinations are auditory commands to perform specific acts (egging on clients to harm themselves or others)

- Defining characteristics a clinician must check:
  - Emotional impact on the client
  - Loudness
  - Frequency
  - Duration
  - Content
  - Degree of hostility
  - Degrees to which client feels driven to follow them

Social Domain

- What reaction does the individual receive when they disclose the behavior?
- Does the person have many tattoos or piercing?
- How does the individual fit into his or her peer group?
- Is there interaction with family, friends, boss and co-workers?
- Is there participation in the therapeutic milieu on an inpatient unit or in a day program?
- Does the individual function at home, at work or in the community?
- Does the individual's religion influence the choice to have tattoos or piercing?
- How does the individual characterize his/her spiritual part of self?
- Has the individual begun to question the role of his/her spiritual beliefs?
- Is the person angry with God?
- Is the individual able to identify a purpose and meaning in his/her life?

MUTILATION ASSESSMENT

General Questions

- What type of self-mutilation is most common for the individual?
- When does it occur?
- What are the environmental or thought cues?
- What types of interventions diminish the drive to self-mutilate?

After the Assessment: Review with the Client

- What I have learned from you indicates that you tend to self-mutilate when:

  1. _____

  2. _____

  3. _____

- Your favorite methods of self-harm include

    1. _____

    2. _____

    3. _____

To Handle Anxiety: What to Tell Clients

To help you handle your anxiety and strong desires to self-harm, we can work together on developing some personal strategies that can help you through hard times.

   Are you willing to work with me on this?

THREAT ASSESSMENT

Often practitioners are asked to make a formal evaluation of a client to determine whether that client is at risk to harm himself or herself or another person. The following materials may be used to determine degree of threat (Callahan, 2008).

THREAT ASSESSMENT REFERRAL FORM
(Kentucky Department of Education, 2000).

If you become concerned that an individual may pose a risk for harming himself or others complete this form by stating your concern, checking the Warning Signs of which you are aware, and explaining items checked. Turn it in directly to the school's principal or designee. In an *imminent* safety threat, notify principal immediately and take immediate action to secure or isolate the individual, and move other students from harm's way.

Individual under concern _____   **Date of birth** _____

Person(s) completing this form _____   **Room/phone** _____

School _____   **Date of referral** _____

I. Reason for Referral (explain your concerns) _____

_____

_____

II. Imminent Warning Signs (when an individual displays Imminent Warning Signs; take immediate action to maintain safety, mobilize law enforcement & appropriate school personnel)

☐ 1. Possession and/or use of firearm or other weapon

☐ 2. Suicide threats or statements

☐ 3. Detailed threats of lethal violence (time, place, method)

☐ 4. Severe rage for seemingly minor reasons

☐ 5. Severe destruction of property

☐ 6. Serious physical fighting with peers, family, others

III. Early Warning Signs (mark items, then elaborate below)

☐ 7. Social withdrawal or lacking interpersonal skills

☐ 8. Excessive feelings of isolation & being alone

☐ 9. Excessive feelings of rejection

☐ 10. Being a victim of violence, teasing, bullying

☐ 11. Feelings of being picked on

☐ 12. Low school interest, poor academic performance

☐ 13. Expressions of violence in writings & drawings

☐ 14. Uncontrolled anger

☐ 15. Patterns of impulsive & chronic, hitting & bullying

☐ 16. History of discipline problems

☐ 17. History of violent, aggressive & antisocial behavior across settings (i.e., fighting, fire setting, cruelty to animals, vandalism, etc., especially begun before age 12)

☐ 18. Intolerance for differences, prejudicial attitudes

☐ 19. Drug & alcohol use

☐ 20. Affiliation with gangs

☐ 21. Inappropriate access, possession, use of firearms

☐ 22. Threats of violence (direct or indirect)

☐ 23. Talking about weapons or bombs

☐ 24. Ruminating over perceived injustices

☐ 25. Seeing self as victim of a particular individual

☐ 26. General statements of distorted, bizarre thoughts

☐ 27. Feelings of being persecuted

☐ 28. Obsession with particular person

☐ 29. Depression

☐ 30. Marked change in appearance

Chart based on U.S. Department of Education's *Early Warning, Timely Response: A Guide to Safe Schools.*

IV. **Explain checked items**; describe known Precipitating Events *(use back if needed)*

_____

_____

_____

V. **Turn in this form** and any materials you may have which may be necessary to conduct a preliminary risk assessment (i.e., writings, notes, printed e-mail or Internet materials, books, drawings, confiscated items, etc.).

Date Received: _____

Clinician or Case Manager assigned to follow referral: _____

THREAT ASSESSMENT WORKSHEET

Coupled with the Referral Form (which addresses Warning Signs), this outline addresses Risk Factors, Precipitating Events, and Stabilizing Factors. The worksheet is designed to provide a concise way to organize known concerns when conducting a preliminary risk assessment and to list relevant school and agency involvement.

Individual under concern _____ **Date of birth** _____

Person(s) completing this form _____

Parent/legal guardian name _____ **Phone** _____

School _____ **Date of referral** _____

I. **School & Agency Involvement (past or present)** To determine if safety concerns have been noted by others. List name, contact information & date of involvement if known:

School Law Enforcement or Discipline Referrals

Special Education, 504, or Under Consideration _____

School-based Mental Health or Social Services _____

Family Resource and Youth Services Center _____

Community Social Services _____

Police, Juvenile Court, Probation Services _____

Community Mental Health Services _____

Current or prior institutionalization or foster care placement _____

Other _____

Comments/concerns expressed by any of the above _____

II. **Risk Factors** (indicate if Observed, Documented, or Suspected; circle O, D, S, respectively)

In possession or has access to weapons (O, D, S) _____

History of impulsive violent or other antisocial behavior (O, D, S) _____

Child abuse/neglect (O, D, S) _____

Isolation or social withdrawal (O, D, S) _____

Domestic violence or other family conflict (O, D, S) _____

Depression, mental illness, medical ailment (O, D, S) (list current medications) _____

Substance abuse or drug trafficking (O, D, S) _____

Fire setting (O, D, S) _____

Bed Wetting (O, D, S) _____

Cruelty to animals (O, D, S) _____

Preoccupation with real or fictional violence (O, D, S) _____

Repeated exposure to violence (desensitization) (O, D, S) _____

Gang involvement or affiliation (O, D, S) _____

Other _____

III. Precipitating Events (recent triggers which may influence violence)

Recent public humiliation/embarrassment (whether instigated by adult or peer) _____

_____

Boyfriend/girlfriend relationship difficulties _____

Death, loss or other traumatic event _____

Highly publicized violent act (such as a school shooting)_____

Family fight or conflict _____

Recent victim of teasing, bullying or abuse _____

Other _____

IV. Stabilizing Factors (factors which may minimize or mitigate likelihood of violence)

Effective parental involvement _____

Involved with mental health; list provider or agency (if known) _____

Social support networks (church, school, social organizations) _____

Close alliance with a supportive adult (counselor, mentor, teacher, minister, etc.) _____

_____

Positive, constructive peer group_____

Appropriate outlets for anger or other strong feelings _____

Positive focus on the future or appropriate future events_____

Other _____

V. Category of Risk (Determine a Risk for Harm Category based on available information)

Imminent	**High**	**Moderate**	**Minor**	**Low/No**

(Date & time of determination _____)

NOTE: Risk For Harm Categories represent a distinct moment in time and may change from hour to hour, and day to day. Following an initial assessment, it is essential to monitor on-going status, to reassess level of risk according to new information, and to document significant changes.

RISK (OR THREAT) ASSESSMENT CONCEPTS

I. Warning Signs: A sign or indicator that causes concern for safety.

   A. Imminent Warning Sign: A sign which indicates that an individual is very close to behaving in a way that is potentially dangerous to self or others. Imminent Warning Signs call for immediate action by school authorities and law enforcement.

   B. Early Warning Signs: Certain behavioral and emotional signs that, when viewed in a context, may signal a troubled individual. Early Warning Signs call for a referral to a school's Threat Assessment Team for assessment.

II. Risk Factors: Historical or background conditions which may influence the potential for violence. These factors may include family history of violence, prior antisocial behavior, mental health background, and various social factors.

III. Precipitating Events: Recent events or "triggers" which may increase potential for violence. These factors may include recent family conflict, rejection from a significant peer, serious conflict with a teacher, etc.

IV. Stabilizing Factors: Support systems or networks in place for an individual which may decrease the likelihood for violence. These factors may include effective parental relationships, positive peer groups, strong relationship with a teacher, counselor or therapist, etc.

V. Threat Assessment: The process of reviewing Warning Signs, Risk Factors, Precipitating Events, and Stabilizing Factors, to determine the Risk for Harm Category and develop an appropriate plan of action.

RISK FOR HARM CATEGORIES

Risk For Harm Categories provide a way for clinicians to determine and assign a level of risk based on a review of Warning Signs, Risk Factors, Precipitating Events, and Stabilizing Factors. Based on level of risk, the Emergency Management Team develops action plans to maintain safety and to help an individual gain access to needed services or interventions. The descriptors following each Category are not an exhaustive list, but are provided as a frame of reference.

Category 1: Imminent Risk for Harm.

An individual is, or is very close to, behaving in a way that is potentially dangerous to self or others. Examples include: detailed threats of lethal violence, suicide threats, possession and/or use of firearms or other weapons, serious physical fighting, etc. Most of these individuals will qualify for immediate hospitalization or arrest. Responses may include: immediate action to secure individual, arrest or hospitalization, facility lock down, security response, parent notification, background or records check, "return to school plans," ongoing case management.

Category 2: High Risk for Harm.

An individual has displayed significant Early Warning Signs, has significant existing Risk Factors and/or Precipitating Events, and has few Stabilizing Factors. May not qualify for hospitalization or arrest at present, but requires referrals for needed services and active case management. Responses may include: immediate action to secure individual, security response, parent notification, psychological consult/evaluation, background check.

Category 3: Moderate Risk for Harm.

An individual has displayed some Early Warning Signs and may have existing Risk Factors or recent Precipitating Events, but also may have some Stabilizing Factors. There may be evidence of internal emotional distress (depression, social withdrawal, etc.) or of intentional infliction of distress on others (bullying, intimidation, seeking to cause fear, etc.). Responses may include: security response, parent notification, psychological consult/evaluation, background or records check, ongoing case management.

Category 4: Minor Risk for Harm.

An individual has displayed minor Early Warning Signs, but assessment reveals little history of serious Risk Factors or dangerous behavior. Stabilizing Factors appear to be reasonably well established. There may be evidence of the unintentional infliction of distress on others (insensitive remarks, "teasing" taken too far, etc.). Responses may include: review of school records, parent notification, psychological consult, security response.

Category 5: Low/No Risk for Harm.

Upon assessment it appears there is insufficient evidence for any risk for harm. Situations under this category can include misunderstandings, poor decision making, false accusations from peers (seeking to get other peers in trouble), etc. Responses may include: investigation of the situation, notification and involvement of others as needed, etc.

BRIEF INTERVIEW OUTLINE
FOR INDIVIDUAL UNDER CONCERN

When interviewing an individual about safety concerns, one method is to ask questions which move from general introduction, to fact finding, to recognition of concerns, to assessing support networks, to developing an outline for next steps. The following questions are not intended to be a scripted interview, but provide a sample structure for the kinds of questions which may need to be asked. Individuals using this outline are encouraged to use their professional judgment and experience, and to broaden or alter the questions. Note, in general it is good to avoid "yes or no" questions.

1. "Seems like you've been having a hard time lately, what's going on?" (*to establish rapport and trust and to open dialog in a non-threatening way*)

2. "What is your understanding of why you have been asked to come to the office?" (*to review factual events*)

3. "What is your understanding of why school staff are concerned?" (*to determine if student is aware of the effect the behavior has on others*)

4. "What has been going on recently with you at school?" (*to look into possible precipitating events such as peer conflict, student/teacher interactions, failing grades, etc.; follow appropriate leads*)

5. "How are things going with your family?" (*to look into events such as recent moves, divorce, deaths or losses, conflict*)

6. "What else is going on with you?" (*to look into events outside of school such as community unrest, threats, police involvement, medical issues, etc.*)

7. "Who do you have to talk to or assist you with this situation?" (to determine what supports or stabilizing factors may be available or in place such as mental health professionals, peer groups, family supports, church groups, etc.)

8. "Given (whatever is going on), what are you planning to do?" or, "What are you thinking about doing?" (*follow-up on appropriate leads, including the level of detail in stated plans, ability to carry out plans, etc.*) **(NOTE: If there is an _IMMINENT RISK_ take immediate action to maintain safety by contacting school security and/or 911).**

9. Close with a statement that describes short term next steps (i.e., "I'll need to contact your parents to talk about . . ." or, "You will be suspended for two days, then we'll . . ."). Try to determine student's affect or mood prior to his/her departure, and alert others if necessary.

Depending on the outcome of the threat assessment, duty to warn calls may be necessary or clinical interventions like hospitalization may be necessary as listed under the risk categories. If the client is at low risk, but upset, clinicians can employ DBT techniques to help a client curb impulsive or acting out behaviors. Acting out behaviors are any behaviors that are harmful to self or others.

USE DBT DISTRACTION

For interventions, you will want to teach Dialectical Behavior Therapy Crisis Survival Skills. Two sets of skills that are Crisis Survival Skills are

- Distract Skills
- Self-Soothing Skills

Distraction Skills (Linehan, 1993)
<u>Distress Tolerance</u>: **ACCEPTS**

> **A**ctivities
>
> **C**ontributing
>
> **C**omparisons
>
> **E**motions
>
> **P**ushing away
>
> **T**houghts
>
> **S**ensations

<u>The "A" in ACCEPTS</u>

> **A**ctivities:
> - Engage in exercise or hobbies;
> - do cleaning;
> - go to events;
> - call or visit a friend;
> - play computer games;
> - go walking; work;
> - play sports;
> - go out to a meal,
> - have a decaf coffee or tea;
> - go fishing;
> - chop wood,
> - do gardening;
> - play pinball.

The "C" in ACCEPTS

Contributing:
- Contribute to someone;
- do volunteer work;
- give something to someone else;
- make something nice for someone else;
- do a surprising, thoughtful thing.

The Second "C" in ACCEPTS

Comparisons:
- Compare yourself to people coping the same as you or not as well as you.
- Compare yourself to those less fortunate than you.
- Watch soap operas.
- Read about disasters, others' suffering

The "E" in ACCEPTS

Emotions:
- Read emotional books or stories, old letters; go to emotional movies; listen to emotional music.
- Be sure the event creates different emotions.
- Ideas: scary movies, joke books, comedies, funny records, religious music, marching songs, "I Am Woman" (Helen Reddy); going to a store and reading funny greeting cards.

The "P" in ACCEPTS

Pushing away:
- Push the situation away by leaving it for a while. Leave the situation mentally.
- Build an imaginary wall between yourself and the situation.
- Push the situation away by blocking it in your mind. Censor ruminating.
- Refuse to think about the painful aspects of the situation.
- Put the pain on a shelf. Box it up and put it away for a while.

The "T" in ACCEPTS

Thoughts:
- Count to 10;
- Count colors in a painting or tree, windows
- Work puzzles;
- Watch TV;
- Read.

The "S" in ACCEPTS

Sensations:
- Hold ice in your hand;
- squeeze a rubber ball very hard;
- stand under a very hard and hot shower;
- listen to very loud music;
- put rubber band on wrist, pull out, and let go.

The Self-Soothing Skills: What to Tell Clients

- A second set of skills that will help you get through tough times.
- You do not want to harm yourself.
- You do not want to make yourself so upset that you get out of control.
- You can learn and practice self-soothing skills.

Self-Soothing Skills (Linehan, 1993)

A way to remember these skills is to think of soothing each of your **FIVE SENSES:**

Vision

Hearing

Smell

Taste

Touch

With Vision:

- Buy one beautiful flower; make one space in a room pretty; light a candle and watch the flame.
- Set a pretty place at the table, using your best things, for a meal.
- Go to a museum with beautiful art. Go sit in the lobby of a beautiful old hotel. Look at nature around you.
- Go out in the middle of the night and watch the stars. Walk in a pretty part of town.
- Fix your nails so they look pretty. Look at beautiful pictures in a book.
- Go to a ballet or other dance performance, or watch one on TV.
- Be mindful of each sight that passes in front of you, not lingering on any.

With Hearing:

- Listen to beautiful or soothing music, or to invigorating and exciting music.
- Pay attention to sounds of nature (waves, birds, rainfall, leaves rustling).
- Sing to your favorite songs.
- Hum a soothing tune.

- Learn to play an instrument.
- Call 800 or other information numbers to hear a human voice.
- Be mindful of any sounds that come your way, letting them go in one ear and out the other.

With *Smell*:

- Use your favorite perfume or lotions, or try them on in the store; spray fragrance in the air; light a scented candle.
- Put lemon oil on your furniture.
- Put potpourri in a bowl in your room.
- Boil cinnamon; bake cookies, cake, or bread.
- Smell the roses.
- Walk in a wooded area and mindfully breathe in the fresh smells of nature.

With *Taste*:

- Have a good meal; have a favorite soothing drink such as herbal tea or hot chocolate (no alcohol); treat yourself to a dessert.
- Put whipped cream on your coffee.
- Sample flavors in an ice cream store.
- Suck on a piece of peppermint candy.
- Chew your favorite gum.
- Get a small quantity of a special food you don't usually spend the money on, such as fresh-squeezed orange juice.
- Really taste the food you eat; eat one thing mindfully.

With *Touch*:

- Take a bubble bath; put clean sheets on the bed. Pet your dog or cat.
- Put creamy lotion on your whole body.
- Put a cold compress on your forehead.
- Sink into a really comfortable chair in your home, or find one in a luxurious hotel lobby.
- Put on a silky blouse, dress, or scarf.
- Try on fur-lined gloves or fur coats in a department store.
- Brush your hair for a long time.
- Hug someone. Experience whatever you are touching; take notice of a soothing touch.

HOMEWORK: USE CHARTS WITH CLIENTS

Distracting Skills

Skill	Mon.	Tue.	Wed.	Thur.	Fri.	Sat.	Sun.
Activity							
Comparison							
Contribution							
Emotion							
Pushing Away							
Thoughts							
Sensations							

Self-Soothing Skills Homework Chart

Senses	Mon.	Tue.	Wed.	Thur.	Fri.	Sat.	Sun.	Harmed
Vision								YES NO
Hearing								YES NO
Smell								YES NO
Taste								YES NO
Touch								YES NO

JOURNALING

Journal thoughts and feelings to explore emotional patterns of when the self mutilation occurs. Be specific.

Date	Type of Mutilation	How I Felt

The clinician and client should go over the journal together.

A goal would be to become aware of negative thoughts that cause increase in anxiety and therefore are a stimulus to increase the possibility of dissociation and possible self-mutilation.

USE THOUGHT RECORDS

Thought records are charts that can help a therapist slow down an injustice collector or a terribly anxious child. Injustice collectors are often teens or preteens who slam into an office and in the first several minutes of therapy tell a therapist *everything* that is wrong, listing fifteen to twenty problems all at once. A terribly anxious child may come through the door overwhelmingly anxious and list seventeen items that are worrying them. A thought record helps you slow down a client and take charge of a therapy session. You inform the client that you only have an hour's session and that you need to help them decide which issue is most pressing so that you both can wisely use the time you are allotted. You would then hand the client a copy of a thought record:

Date	Situation	Thought	Feeling	Behavior Outcome

USE SCHEMA CHANGE METHODS

Schema are deep cognitive structures that enable an individual to interpret his or her experiences in a meaningful way (Beck, 1976). In Beck's cognitive theory, depressed clients have distorted, negative schema that when activated by life events give rise to negative automatic thoughts (e.g., "I can't do this"), problematic moods (e.g., depression), and maladaptive behaviors (e.g., procrastination).

BECK'S THEORY

Beck described four types of schema: views of self, others, world, and future. The theory proposes that depressed clients hold negative, distorted views

- of themselves (worthless, useless, a loser, bad, defective, unlovable, second rate, a piece of garbage),
- others (uncaring, attacking, critical, rejecting),
- the world (burdensome, dark and unforgiving, bleak, ungratifying, punishing), and
- the future (hopeless, unrewarding, futile).

Clinically, it may not be necessary (or possible) to work on all of the client's maladaptive schema, so therapeutic work should focus on the one or two that cause the most problems for the client

THE POSITIVE DATA LOG

This is one schema change method. To use it, you need to understand three principles about how your clients think.

1. A given schema can be activated in many situations

2. Schema include both positive and negative information

3. Schema determine what people *notice*, *attend to*, and *remember*

Schema Activation

A person who believes "I'm incompetent" can experience emotional, behavioral, and cognitive reactions when this schema is activated in multiple diverse situations.

A teenager's incompetence schema can be activated

- when a friend does not return his telephone call promptly,
- in heavy traffic when an impatient driver honks at him, and
- at home after a shopping trip when he discovers the expensive shirt he just bought does not fit properly.

This can lead to distressing thoughts which in turn can lead to suicidal thoughts or self-mutilation

Positive and Negative Information

From the information-processing literature, we know that schema are multidimensional and contain both positive and negative information (for a review, *see* Segal, 1988). The teenager who feels incompetent in the situations just described can feel highly competent when he receives a compliment from a parent, teacher or friend.

Padesky (1996) called the schema that oppose the negative schema "balancing schema." According to cognitive theory, problems arise both when negative schema are too strong or activated too often and when balancing or positive schema are too weak or activated too infrequently (Beck, 1976).

Clinicians Must

As you go over thought records and journals, you need to determine if the client has balancing thoughts and if negative schema are too strong and appear too often. You need to know if positive schema are weak or if positive thoughts appear at all.

What Does Your Client Notice?

Depressed individuals remember fewer and less specific positive autobiographical memories and more specific negative memories.

They also have a bias to attend to negative information (Williams, 1992).

There is some evidence that these deficits persist in vulnerable individuals, even when they recover from depression (for a review, see Gotlib & Krasnoperova, 1998).

HOW THE LOG WORKS

The Positive Data Log capitalizes on all three of these observations about schema.

The Positive Data Log teaches the client

- to notice the multiple situations in which schema are activated,
- helps the client strengthen the positive or balancing schema, and
- helps the client notice and overcome biases in processing information driven by schema.

Guidelines: Using a Positive Data Log

Provide a rationale. Keeping a Positive Data Log is a difficult task because individuals often fail to perceive or remember information that contradicts their negative schema.

Identify balancing schema. Because the client is asked to record evidence in support of his or her positive or balancing schema, it is important to be certain the balancing schema is clear and specific. Use the client's words for greater impact.

Start the Positive Data Log during the session. Spend some time starting the Positive Data Log during the session and demonstrating how to use the Positive Data Log form.

<u>*Instruct clients to enter evidence on the Positive Data Log as soon as possible.*</u> Explain to clients that it is important that they enter evidence on the Positive Data Log as soon as they observe it. If they wait until the end of the day or even 1 or 2 hours after to enter the evidence, the evidence may be lost because the client will forget it, minimize it, or discount it.

POSITIVE DATA LOG

Instructions: Describe your maladaptive schema and alternative schema in the space provided. Then write down each piece of evidence in support of your alternative schema and the date and time when you observed the evidence. Be as specific as you can. For example, in your maladaptive state you might tell yourself, "No one likes me because no one talked to me today. Then think of a situation where someone did talk to you. Be very specific. For example in the alternative spot you might write: "Someone said something nice to me," but be specific and write "Tom said he liked the shoes I was wearing." Remember, you are to write down all evidence in support of your alternative schema, regardless of how small or insignificant you might think it is.

Maladaptive schema:

_____

_____

Alternative schema:

_____

_____

Then you have the client keep a record of positive thinking and events.

Date	Evidence of Positive Thinking & Events

Next

Whenever a negative schema arises,

- you pull out the positive data log,
- actively help the client challenge the negative thought,
- look for positives in life,
- record them, and
- insist the client practice positive thoughts.

Example

Maladaptive Schema: "Everybody hates me."

Disputing from the clinician: "That is an interesting statement. I am here with you today. Do you believe that I hate you? The receptionist called to tell me you were here. Does she hate you? Can you name some other person who might not hate you? What evidence do we have that the person you named does not hate you?"

You would write down what that evidence is in the positive data log.

Next

You would help the client rewrite his/her maladaptive schema into an alternative schema. With a self-mutilating client, you will want to take a few other steps. You would ask, "When you tell yourself that everyone hates you, what do you do next?"

If self-mutilating behavior follows, ask the client what s/he could do instead of cutting, burning, or hurting himself or herself?

Move the Client into Action

Contract:

The next time I say to myself, "Everyone hates me" I will:

1. pull out my positive data log

2. focus on the alternative schema

3. use a distracting or self-soothing skill

The skill I will use is _____

_____

_____

Signed   *Date*

This Takes Work

It will have taken your client a long time to develop his/her cognitive behavior pattern, and it takes a lot of practice to change this pattern.

RATIONAL EMOTIVE IMAGING

Imagery

- Imagine very relaxing scenes.
- Imagine a secret room within yourself, seeing how it is decorated.
- Go into the secret room whenever you feel very threatened. Close the door on anything that can hurt you.
- Imagine everything going well. Imagine coping well.
- Make up a fantasy world that is calming and beautiful and let your mind go with it.
- Imagine hurtful emotions draining out of you like water out of a pipe.

Teaching Distraction with Guided Imagery

Place the client in a quiet, calm environment that is free from other distractions such as noise, strong light, or extraneous conversation. Ask him or her to select a place that has been conducive to rest and peace in the past. Then, ask the client to close his or her eyes, if desired, and to imagine that peaceful place. Ask the client to describe the place in terms of its appearances its odors if appropriate, and other sensual characteristics such as its temperature. Use a quiet, subdued tone of voice to avoid interrupting the mood that is being established.

Should the client identify a place such as the beach, you can prompt responses with such non-threatening questions as

- What does the sky look like?
- What color is the sky? Is the air warm?
- How does the warm sand feel to your body?
- Are you alone on the beach?
- Tell me how the water feels to your foot.
- Tell me more about the things that you think and do at the beach." (All of these questions require that the client focus on the place that is being described.)

Gradually, his or her focus on the stressful event is weakened, resulting in a temporary diminution of anxiety. Relaxation occurs as a result of associations with the non-threatening and calming beach.

Change the Thought

Whenever the client tells himself that everyone hates him/her, have the client use the imagery you and s/he has devised to calm down and move into a safe space where there is no self-harming behavior.

Have the client practice imagery 10 times a day.

Problem Solving Skills

These specific steps include:

1. problem definition;
2. listen;
3. brainstorm for solutions;
4. list the options;
5. weigh the options;
6. select a solution;
7. implement the solution;
8. evaluate the results.

Bibliotherapy

Alderman, Tracy—*The Scarred Soul*
Strong, Marilee—*A Bright Red Scream*
Conterio, Karen & Lader, Wendy—*Bodily Harm*
Walsh, Barent—*Self Mutilation: Theory, Research and Treatment*

Websites

Have clients go to websites like

www.healthyplaces.com/communities/self-injury/site
www.selfinjury.com
www.bangordailynews.com
theguide.fmhi.usf.edu (Youth Suicide School-Based Prevention Guide)
www.afsp.org (American Foundation for Suicide Prevention
www.sprc.org (Suicide Prevention Resource Center)
www.spanusa.org (Suicide Prevention Advocacy Network)
www.preventing suicide.com (Preventing Suicide Network)
www.nopcas (National Association for People of Color Against Suicide)
www.med.uio.no/iasp/ (International Association for Suicide Prevention

Hotlines

National Adolescent Suicide Hotline—800 621-4000

The Trevor Helpline for gay and lesbian youths—800 850-8078

Youth Crisis Hotline—800 HIT-HOME (448-4663)

The Befrienders Worldwide—www.suicide-helplines.org./index.html

National Suicide 24-hour Free Helplines:

National Hopeline Network—1-800-SUICIDE

National Suicide Prevention Lifeline—1-800-273-TALK

Center for Elderly Suicide Prevention—1-800-971-0016

Resources

American Self-Harm Information Clearinghouse: www.selfinjury.org

SAFE Alternatives (Self Abuse Finally Ends): A treatment approach and professional network. 800 DON'T-CUT (366-8288)

Suicide Data Bank Project: Therapists who have lost a client to suicide can discuss their case with experts and contribute to research. Call 1-888-333-2377, ext 15

American Foundation for Suicide Prevention: www.afsp.org

Help Prevent Suicide: 1-800-SUICIDE

American Association of Suicidology: 1-800-273-TALK (8255)

With children and adolescents I suggest that you use a paper "No Harm" contract that you have the client sign.

NO-HARM CONTRACT

I, _____, agree not to harm myself in any way, attempt to kill myself, or kill myself during the period from _____ to _____, (the time of my next appointment).

I agree that, for any reason, if the appointed session is postponed, canceled, etc., that this time period is extended until the next direct meeting with my counselor. In this period of time, I agree to care for myself, to eat well, and to get enough sleep each night.

I agree to make social/family contact with the following individuals:

_____   _____

_____   _____

_____   _____

_____   _____

I agree to rid my presence of all things I could use to harm or kill myself. I agree that, if I am having a rough time and come to a point where I may break any of these promises, I will call and make significant contact with any of the following individuals:

_____ at: # _____

_____ at: # _____

_____ at: # _____

Or, if I cannot contact these individuals, I will immediately call the Suicide Crisis Hotline at: # _____

I agree that these conditions are important, worth doing, and that this is a contract I am willing to make and keep. By my word and honor, I intend to keep this contract.

Signed _____ Date _____

Witnessed by _____ Date _____

Never Accept a No Harm Contract as evidence that the client absolutely will not harm himself or herself!

CONTRACTING FOR SAFETY

Do not use "no-harm contracts" for the following patients:

- Agitated
- Psychotic
- Impulsive
- Under the influence of an intoxicating substance

Contracts are dependent on the relationship between the patient and the health care provider and they are not recommended for use in ER or newly admitted patients. Develop contingency plans if contract conditions cannot be kept.

CHAPTER 3

Emotional Vulnerability

Emotional vulnerability is a pattern of pervasive difficulties in regulating negative emotions, including

- high sensitivity to negative emotional stimuli,
- high emotion intensity, and
- slow return to emotional baseline, as well as awareness and experience of emotional vulnerability.

This may include a tendency to blame the social environment for unrealistic expectations and demands.

PARENTS OR ADULTS WHO BRING IN "PROBLEM YOUTHS"

When parents or adults bring in a young person they want you to fix, they will often exclaim that the kid is a problem and that they have done everything to fix this kid. Telling a therapist that the child or adolescent is a problem is normally not helpful. A clinician needs to know exactly what an adult means when the adult characterizes the youth as a problem. A systematic and clarifying tool for this situation is the use of a functional assessment. While there is much information on this type of assessment, one book (O'Neill, Homer, Albin, Sprague, Storey, & Newton, 2006) in particular is helpful.

A short modified function assessment form can be helpful to clinicians. DBT therapists use verbal chain analysis as a tool in therapy, but with children and adolescents a functional analysis may be more useful. Here is a protocol for Functional Analysis.

FUNCTIONAL ASSESSMENT INTERVIEW (FAI)

Person of concern: _____ Age: _____ Sex: M F

Date of interview: _____ Interviewer: _____

Respondents: _____

_____

A. Describe the Behaviors:

1. For each of the behaviors of concern, define the topography (how is it performed), frequency (how often it occurs per day, week, or month), duration (how long it lasts when it occurs), and intensity (how damaging or destructive the behaviors are when they occur).

Behavior	Topography	Frequency	Duration	Intensity
a.				
b.				
c.				
d.				
e.				
f.				
g.				
h.				
i.				
j.				
k.				

2. Which of the behaviors described above are likely to occur together in some way? Do they occur about the same time? In some kind of predictable sequence or "chain"? In response to the same type of situation?

_____

_____

_____

_____

B. Define Ecological Events (setting events) that predict or set up the problem behaviors.

1. What medications is the person taking (if any), and how do you believe these may affect his or her behavior?

   _____

   _____

   _____

2. What medical or physical conditions (if any) does the person experience that may affect his or her behavior (e.g. asthma, allergies, rashes, sinus infections, seizures, problems related to menstruation)?

   _____

   _____

   _____

3. Describe the sleep pattern of the individual and the extent to which these patterns may affect his or her behavior.

   _____

   _____

   _____

4. Describe the eating routines and diet of the person and the extent to which these may affect his or her behavior.

   _____

   _____

   _____

5a. Briefly list below the person's typical daily schedule of activities (Check the circles by those activities the person enjoys and those activities most associated with problems)?

Enjoys	Problems		Enjoys	Problems	
○	○	6:00 am _____	○	○	2:00 pm _____
○	○	7:00 am _____	○	○	3:00 pm _____
○	○	8:00 am _____	○	○	4:00 pm _____
○	○	9:00 am _____	○	○	5:00 pm _____
○	○	10:00 am _____	○	○	6:00 pm _____
○	○	11:00 am _____	○	○	7:00 pm _____
○	○	12:00 pm _____	○	○	8:00 pm _____
○	○	1:00 pm _____	○	○	9:00 pm _____

5b To what extent are the activities on the daily schedule predictable for the person, with regard to what will be happening, when it will occur, with whom, and for how long?

_____

_____

_____

5c To what extent does the person have the opportunity during the day to make choices about his or her activities and reinforcing events? (E.g., food, clothing, social companions, leisure activities)

_____

_____

_____

6. How many other persons are typically around the individual at home, school, or work (including staff, classmates, and housemates)? Does the person typically seem bothered in situations that are more crowded and noisy?

_____

_____

_____

7. What is the pattern of staffing support that the person receives in home, school, work, and other settings (E.g. 1:1, 2:1)? Do you believe that the number of staff, the training of staff or their social interactions with the person affect the problem behaviors?

_____

_____

_____

C. DEFINE SPECIFIC IMMEDIATELY ANTECEDENT EVENTS THAT PREDICT WHEN THE BEHAVIORS ARE LIKELY AND NOT LIKELY TO OCCUR.

1. *Times of Day: When are the behaviors most and least likely to happen?*

Most likely: _____

_____

Least likely: _____

_____

2. *Settings: Where are the behaviors most and least likely to happen?*

    Most likely: _____

    _____

    Least likely: _____

    _____

3. *People: With whom are the behaviors most and least likely to happen?*

    Most likely: _____

    _____

    Least likely: _____

    _____

4. *Activity: What activities are most and least likely to produce the behaviors?*

    Most likely: _____

    _____

    Least likely: _____

    _____

5. Are there particular or idiosyncratic situations or events not listed above that sometimes seem to "set off" the behaviors, such as particular demands, noises, lights, clothing?

    _____

    _____

    _____

6. What *one thing* could you do that would most likely make the undesirable behaviors occur?

    _____

    _____

    _____

7. Briefly describe how the person's behavior would be affected if . . .

    a. You asked him or her to perform a difficult task.

    _____

    _____

    b. You interrupted a desired activity such as eating ice cream or watching TV.

    _____

    _____

c. You unexpectedly changed his or her typical routine or schedule of activities.

_____

_____

d. She or he wanted something but wasn't able to get it (e.g. a food item up on a shelf).

_____

_____

e. You didn't pay attention to the person or left her or him alone for a while (e.g. 15 minutes).

_____

_____

D. IDENTIFY THE CONSEQUENCES OR OUTCOMES OF THE PROBLEM BEHAVIORS THAT MAY BE MAINTAINING THEM (I.E. THE FUNCTIONS THEY SERVE FOR THE PERSON IN PARTICULAR SITUATIONS).

1. Think of each of the behaviors listed in Section A, and try to identify the specific consequences or outcomes the person gets when the behaviors occur in different situations.

Behavior	Particular Situations	What exactly does she or he get?	What exactly does she or he avoid?
a.			
b.			
c.			
d.			
e.			
f.			
g.			
h.			
i.			
j.			
k.			

E. CONSIDER THE OVERALL EFFICIENCY OF THE PROBLEM BEHAVIORS, EFFICIENCY IS THE COMBINED RESULT OF (a) HOW MUCH PHYSICAL EFFORT IS REQUIRED, (b), HOW OFTEN THE BEHAVIOR IS PERFORMED BEFORE IT IS REWARDED, AND (C) HOW LONG THE PERSON MUST WAIT TO GET THE REWARD.

	Low efficiency				High efficiency
_____	1	2	3	4	5
_____	1	2	3	4	5
_____	1	2	3	4	5
_____	1	2	3	4	5
_____	1	2	3	4	5

F. WHAT FUNCTIONAL ALTERNATIVE BEHAVIORS DOES THE PERSON ALREADY KNOW HOW TO DO?

What socially appropriate behaviors or skills can the person already performs that may generate the same outcomes or reinforcers produced by the problem behaviors?

_____

G. WHAT ARE THE PRIMARY WAYS THE PERSON COMMUNICATES WITH OTHER PEOPLE?

1. What are the general expressive communication strategies used by or available to the person? These might include vocal speech, signs/gestures, communication boards/books, or electronic devices. How consistently are the strategies used?

_____

_____

2. On the following chart, indicate the behaviors the person uses to achieve the communicative outcomes listed:

Communicative Functions	Complex Speech	Multiple-word phrases	One word utterances	Echolalia	Other vocalizations	Complex signing	Single signs	Pointing	Leading	Shakes head	Grabs/reaches	Increased movement	Moves close to you	Moves away or leaves	Fixed gaze	Facial expression	Aggression	Self-injury	Other
Request attention																			
Request help																			
Request preferred food/objects/activities																			
Request break																			
Shows you something or some place																			
Indicate physical pain (headache, illness)																			
Indicate confusion or unhappiness																			
Protest or reject a situation or activity																			

3. With regard to the person's receptive communication, or ability to understand mother persons . . .

   a. Does the person follow spoken requests or instructions? If so, approximately how many? (List if only a few).

   b. Does the person respond to signed or gestural requests or instructions? If so, approximately how many? (List if only a few).

   c. Is the person able to imitate if you provide physical models for various tasks or activities? (List if only a few).

   d. How does the person typically indicate yes or no when asked if she or he wants something, wants to go somewhere, and so on?

H. WHAT ARE THINGS YOU SHOULD DO AND THINGS YOU SHOULD AVOID IN WORKING WITH AND SUPPORTING THIS PERSON?

1. What things can you do to improve the likelihood that a teaching session or other action will go well with this person?

    _____

    _____

2. What things should you avoid that might interfere with or disrupt a teaching session or activity with this person?

    _____

    _____

I. WHAT ARE THINGS THE PERSON LIKES AND ARE REINFORCING FOR HIM OR HER?

1. Food items: _____

2. Toys and objects: _____

3. Activities at home: _____

4. Activities/outings in the community: _____

    Others: _____

J. WHAT DO YOU KNOW ABOUT THE HISTORY OF THE UNDESIRABLE BEHAVIORS, THE PROGRAMS THAT HAVE BEEN ATTEMPTED TO DECREASE OR ELIMINATE THEM, AND THE EFFECTS OF THOSE PROGRAMS?

Behavior	How long has this been a problem	Programs	Effects
1.			
2.			
3.			
4.			
5.			
6.			
7.			
8.			
9.			

K. DEVELOP SUMMARY STATEMENTS FOR EACH MAJOR PREDICTOR AND/OR CONSEQUENCE

Distant Setting Event	Immediate Antecedent (Predictor)	Problem Behavior	Maintaining Consequences
Example: More likely if no breakfast.	Example: When Curtis is asked to complete difficult or non-preferred math and reading tasks.	Example: He will yell obscenities and/or throw objects.	Example: In order to escape from the tasks.

For each problem identified, list the problem and develop a behavioral support plan with interventions chosen to eliminate or reduce the problem:

Problem **Intervention**

_____

_____

_____

_____

_____

_____

AFTER DEFINING PROBLEMS

Linehan (1995) noted that one problem with traditional therapy is that often traditional therapies push for change in clients. Often DBT training begins with teaching mindfulness to clients. Just what *is* mindfulness?

Dialectical Behavior Therapy

Mindfulness and principles derived from Zen philosophy came to form an important part of DBT because of the perceived limitations of traditional cognitive and behavioral approaches for the treatment of BPD .

Linehan recognized that a major shortcoming of these approaches was their heavy emphasis on change, which was experienced as invalidating by patients with BPD. To effectively engage these patients, more attention needed to be paid to nurturing the therapeutic relationship. Linehan modified traditional cognitive and behavioral treatment by placing a greater emphasis on validation and acceptance.

DBT and Mindfulness

As a core skill, mindfulness is taught in DBT. Mindfulness skills make up the first of 4 skills modules and involve psychological and behavioral versions of meditative techniques for cultivating awareness and acceptance.

Patients learn how to recognize different states of mind along with methods for achieving mindfulness ("what" skills) and practicing mindfulness ("how" skills).

The Practice of Mindfulness

Central to this process is the experience of mindfulness which Jon Kabat-Zinn defines as "paying attention on purpose in the present moment non-judgmentally."

This involves learning a way of noticing what is happening in your body, as well as what is on your mind, including the extent to which your mind may be disturbed by troubling thought patterns that seem impossible to shut off:

A Problem

A problem that borderline clients (especially teenagers) have is that they get upset and stay upset. They become obsessed with their thinking, their anger, the way they have been "wronged in life" and they cannot let go of this. They need help with their state of mind—they need to be taught mindfulness skills. To let go, they have to learn to watch.

Yes

Letting go involves a practice that is like learning to sit by the bank of the river of your emotions and letting them flow, coming and going, without getting caught up in them or in the occasional torrent.

DBT Distinguishes

DBT therapists often discuss two types of minds:

- The DOING MIND and
- The BEING MIND

With mindfulness we deliberately focus on the *Being Mind*. We are primarily in *Doing Mind* most of the time. *Doing Mind* is necessary, but there is more to the world than analysis. By being caught up in *Doing Mind*, we miss important pieces of information that could change our experience of the world

The *Doing Mind*

- approaches knowledge "from the head"
- is about information and facts
- is oriented to the future
- plans behavior and is "rational" rather than "emotional"

The *Being Mind*

- observes and records, does not analyze
- watches and senses
- observes facts but does not process them
- is not "doing" anything with the input

Homework

Practice Mindful Breathing five times each day

- Breathe slowly, deeply counting to 10 by thousands
- Pause between each inhale and exhale
- Watch your breath enter and exit
- Feel all motions associated with your breathing
- Bring your mind gently back each time it wanders

As a clinician gives the homework assignment, he or she should identify obstacles to homework and tell clients:

- When you come back and I asked if you practiced your breathing you are likely to tell me that you forgot.
- When you come back and I asked if you practiced your breathing you are likely to tell me that you did not have enough time.
- When you come back and I asked if you practiced your breathing you are likely to tell me that you had no quiet place to practice.
- When you come back and I asked if you practiced your breathing you are likely to become judgmental of technique/self.

- What I need for you to do is simply try this because it will allow you to let go of anger, injustice and worry just for a few minutes and learn how to just be.

Mindfulness Is Easy

Tell clients that the breathing is something that you can do anytime anywhere. Since the objective is to simply watch and welcome experience, there is no "effort" to apply to what you are watching. There is no time requirement; you can do it for 5 minutes or 45 minutes, as long as you like. Once you begin practicing regularly, there is a sense of self-empowerment that is enriching.

Mindfulness Is Hard

We have trained our minds, over time, to divert attention, scan briefly, and "leave" experience rather than sustain attention to it. This is difficult to overcome, and requires practice. With emotional pain, it is difficult to simply watch experience rather than try to stop it. The mind is an "active" process that wants to shift and get lost in many experiences, not just one.

MINDFULNESS AS OBSERVATION

Aim: To teach a child the practice of mindfulness.

Materials: Provide the child with a small notebook and pen or pencil.

Method: For a child or teen, ask him or her to think of himself or herself as an alien and think of me as the mother alien. His or her mission is to go to Earth and describe objects so that we can learn about Earth.

Give the child a notebook that can be used to record information.

You tell the child or teen, "You are part of an exploratory mission, and your assignment is simply to bring back observations (descriptions), rather than conclusions (analyses)."

ONE MIND

Aim: To teach a teen the elements of mindfulness: using Linehan's (1993b) acronym ONE MIND.

Materials: Verbal interaction. Simply explain that the words "one mind" each contain a letter that explains the how to become mindful and to pay attention to things in the world following each letter.

One thing at a time.
Now.
Environment: What is happening out there?

Moment. Immediate.
Increase senses: touch, taste, vision, hearing
No judgment. Purpose is not to analyze or form conclusions.
Depict without attempting to influence.

One thing

- Pay attention to only one thing at a time.
- Stick with your observation of the one thing as long as you can.
- Keep watching the one thing.
- When you find your mind wandering to other topics or thoughts, as it inevitably will, gently bring your focus of attention back.

Now

- Mindfulness is watching, observing, experiencing rather than "thinking about something" that happened in the past or you anticipate in the future.
- Mindfulness pays attention to something happening now.

Moment

- Immediacy. The event or object being mindfully observed is in the here and now.
- Each moment offers a new opportunity to observe how the event or object is.

Increase Senses

- Taste
- Touch
- Vision
- Hearing
- Smell

No Judgment

- The purpose is not to evaluate if we like something or don't like something.
- The purpose is not to assess our attitude about it.
- We are not thinking about it, we are watching it.

Depict

- Use your words to activate mindfulness.
- Your words mirror or create a map of that which you watch.
- Your words should not limit or embellish (change) that which is being watched.

Mindfulness is NOT

- Simply thinking about something intently.
- Analysis, processing, or judging something.
- Being on "automatic pilot" and letting your mind wander from topic to topic.
- Obsessing or ruminating on something for long periods of time.
- Free association, letting whatever comes to mind come to mind.

WORRY WARTS: A TEACHING EXERCISE FOR YOUNG PEOPLE

Aim: To teach young people to reduce worries or other behaviors.

Structure of the Sessions:

Make a Worry Warts Wastebasket and place it near the door.

Prepare a room by marking "personal spaces" on the floor with masking tape.

Place a floor mat and a folder in each space.

Prepare folders with group rules (what goes on in group stays in group), a sheet of stickers, "worry" paper, and a pencil.

Place one chair at the back of the room (so a child can choose to "sit out" of any activity).

Have the kids come into the room and sit on a mat.

Teach the children deep breathing (hold breath, count to ten by thousands, exhale counting to ten by thousands).

    Breathe slowly, deeply

    Pause between each inhale and exhale

    Watch your breath enter and exit

    Feel all motions associated with your breathing

Then have the children describe any worries they have on paper, using the stickers, markers, pens—depicting their most pressing worries for that day any way they would like. (5 minutes)

Do the breathing exercise again.

For five minutes have the children share the worries they have depicted with the other group members.

Do the breathing exercise again.

Then the children are invited to throw the paper in the Worry Warts Wastebasket.

After that, they are asked to "just be" while we do the breathing exercise one last time.

Then the children line up to file out of the room and ask them to place their worry papers in the Worry Warts Basket. They are told they can leave their worries in the Worry Warts Basket or they can reclaim their worries if they wish. Most do not.

A variation of this is to use fears, anger, etc. You would create a fearless basket or a "mads" basket first. The children would list all their fears, share them and throw them away or they would list everything they are mad about and throw their "mads" away.

MINDFULNESS WITH A RAISIN: MINDFUL EATING.

Aim: To practice mindful eating using a single raisin

Structure of the Sessions:

As children enter the room, they remove their shoes, sit down in their own space, and they are given a raisin.

They are told, "Each of you have an object. Hold this object in your hand. Look at it carefully. When you are ready, I invite you to explore this object with all of your senses. "

What color is your object?

Does it change color at different places?

What does the surface texture look like?

Does the object look dry or moist? Is the shape even on all sides?

Feel your object.

Is it soft or hard?

Do the ridges form a pattern?

Is the texture the same all over the object?

Does it smell?

Place the object in your mouth. How does your tongue connect with the object? Does it feel different in different parts of your mouth?

Is there any taste before you bite into it? Any smell? Does the texture change the longer you hold it in your mouth?

I invite you to observe your thoughts and expectations.

Are you looking forward to swallowing the object and eating another, or fully enjoying the experience of the one that is now in your mouth?

When you are ready, gently bite the object.

What are the flavors as they are released from the skin of the object?

Do the taste and texture of the inside of the object differ from the outside? Is there a difference in moistness or flavor?

Are the sensations different in different parts of your mouth? As you slowly chew the object, note each sensation.

As you swallow it, can you feel the sensation as it slides down your throat?

Can you follow it all the way down to your stomach?

Do you have any leftover sensations in your mouth? Is there a different taste or flavor in your mouth now?

Are your thoughts and sensations still with your immediate experience of eating this object or have they moved elsewhere?

Mindfulness vs Worry

You would tell your clients that by focusing so intently on awareness, that they can focus their mind on something other than worry, fear, anger, injustice and that they can just "be" in the moment. They can let their worries (fear, anger. etc.) overwhelm them or they can free themselves and leave their *Doing Mind* to move into their *Being Mind.*

MINDFULNESS IN EVERYDAY LIFE

Aim: To teach teens how to be focus on the present being aware of elements in the moment.

Method: Participants were encouraged to discover their own ways to practice mindfulness at home, which supports the generalization of mindfulness to daily life.

Invite discussion of their daily experiences of mindfulness.

For example, the children practiced mindful touch at home:

How does your own skin feel? Explore your own hand.

Ask one of your friends or family members if you can touch the skin on their hand and then compare it to your own.

How do they feet different?

Is one softer than the other? Warm? Cool? Smooth? Rough? Silky?

Close your eyes and feel the different textures of your clothes.

Note how your T-shirt feels that may be different from your jeans.

How about your sweater or jacket?

Go around your home and touch everyday objects.

A tennis ball can feet kind of furry and the side of a pen can feel really smooth.

Pillows are often soft and squishy.

Are you alert to when you are judging what you touch rather than just observing and describing the object?

Have each group member discuss his or her experiences at being mindful.

Mindfulness is just one DBT skill that can be used to teach a child that he or she can learn to let go. Other skills that can be taught are relaxation methods that a child can use to reduce high intensity and slow return to baseline.

IMPLEMENT RELAXATION FOR TEENS

Tell the client:

- Choose a quiet, comfortable location where you will not be disturbed for 20 to 30 minutes.
- Your position may be lying or sitting, but all parts of your body should be supported, including your head.
- Wear loose clothing, taking off restrictive items, such as glasses and shoes.
- Begin by closing your eyes and clearing your mind.
- Moving from head to toe, focus on each part of your body and assess the level of tension.
- Visualize each group of muscles as heavy and relaxed.
- Take two or three slow abdominal breaths, pausing briefly in between each breath. Imagine the tension flowing from your body.

Each muscle group listed below should be tightened (or tensed isometrically) for 5 to 10 seconds and then abruptly released, visualizing this group of muscles as heavy, limp, and relaxed for 15 to 20 seconds before tightening the next group of muscles. There are several methods to tighten each muscle group and suggestions are provided below. Each muscle group may be tightened two to three times until relaxed. Do not over tighten or strain. You should not experience pain.

- Hands (tighten by making fists)
- Biceps (tighten by drawing forearms up and "making a muscle")
- Triceps (extend forearms straight, locking elbows)
- Face (grimace, tightly shutting mouth and eyes)
- Face (open mouth wide and raise eyebrows)
- Neck (pull head forward to chest and tighten neck muscles)
- Shoulders (raise shoulders toward ears)
- Shoulders (push shoulders back as if touching them together)
- Chest (take a deep breath and hold for 10 seconds)
- Stomach (suck in your abdominal muscles)
- Buttocks (pull buttocks together)
- Thighs (straighten legs and squeeze muscles in thighs and hips)
- Leg calves (pull toes carefully toward you, avoid cramps)
- Feet (curl toes downward and point toes away from your body)
- Finally, repeat several deep abdominal breaths and mentally check your body for tension. Rest comfortably for several minutes, breathing normally, and visualize your body as warm and relaxed. Get up slowly when you are finished.

BREATHING TO RELAX

Breathing Exercises

Clients should be instructed to:

1. Practice at times when they are not overanxious.

2. Begin by breathing in slowly through the nose counting to four, then hold the breath for a count of four.

3. Exhale slowly through pursed lips to a count of four, and then rest for a count of four (no breath).

4. Take two normal breaths and repeat the sequence.

<u>Breathing Control:</u> Hyperventilation is a common symptom for many individuals who experience panic. Unfortunately, hyperventilation usually increases CO_2 content in the body and, for some individuals, increases the severity of the symptoms. Assisting patients to learn breathing control can be an extremely helpful tool. Often they are unaware that when they become anxious they begin breathing in a very shallow manner that uses only the chest cavity. Helping them to focus on their breathing and identify the rate, pattern, and depth is an important first step. If their breathing is rapid and shallow, reassure the patient that exercise and breathing practice can help change their breathing pattern.

DEEPER BREATHING

Assist the client in practicing abdominal breathing by performing the following exercises:

1. Instruct the individual to place her hand on the abdomen just beneath the rib cage and inhale slowly through the nose, attempting to fill the "bottom" of the lungs. This focuses attention on breathing deeply.

2. Instruct the client to observe that when she is breathing deeply, the hand on the abdomen will actually rise and the diaphragm moves down.

3. After she seems to understand this process, ask the client to inhale slowly through the nose counting to five, then pause, and then exhale slowly counting to five, moving the air out through pursed lips.

4. Direct the attention as she exhales, to feel the muscles relax, focusing on "letting go."

5. Repeat the deep abdominal breathing for 10 breaths, pausing between each inhale and exhale and counting slowly. If she begins to feel light-headed, instruct the individual to stop for 30 seconds, breathe normally, and then start again.

6. She should stop between each round of 10 and monitor normal breathing for 30 seconds.

7. This series of 10 slow abdominal breaths, followed by 30 seconds of normal breathing, should be repeated for 3 to 5 minutes.

8. Assist the client in establishing a time for daily practice of abdominal breathing. Abdominal breathing may also be used to interrupt an episode of panic as it begins.

IMPLEMENT RELAXATION FOR CHILDREN
Progressive Muscle Relaxation for Children (Holistic Psychology)

Directions: Use the following script to help a child relax.

Today we're going to practice some special kinds of exercises called relaxation exercises. These exercises help you to learn how to relax when you're feeling up-tight and help you get rid of those butterflies-in-your-stomach kinds of feelings. They're also kind of neat because you can learn how to do some of them without anyone really noticing.

In order for you to get the best feelings from these exercises, there are some rules you must follow. First, you must do exactly what I say, even if it seems kind of silly. Second, you must try hard to do what I say. Third, you must pay attention to your body. Throughout these exercises, pay attention to how your muscles feel when they are tight and when they are loose and relaxed. And fourth, you must practice. The more you practice, the more relaxed you can get. Do you have any questions? Are you ready to begin? Okay, first, get as comfortable as you can in your chair. Sit back, get both feet on the floor, and just let your arms hang loose. That's fine. Now close your eyes and don't open them until I say to. Remember to follow my instructions very carefully, try hard, and pay attention to your body. Here we go.

Hands and Arms: Pretend you have a whole lemon in your left hand. Now squeeze it hard. Try to squeeze all the juice out. Feel the tightness in your hand and arm as you squeeze. Now drop the lemon. Notice how your muscles feel when they are relaxed. Take another lemon and squeeze. Try to squeeze this one harder than you did the first one. That's right. Real hard. Now drop the lemon and relax. See how much better your hand and arm feel when they are relaxed. Once again, take a lemon in your left hand and squeeze all the juice out. Don't leave a single drop. Squeeze hard. Good. Now relax and let the lemon fall from your hand. (Repeat the process for the right hand and arm.)

Arms and Shoulders: Pretend you are a furry, lazy cat. You want to stretch. Stretch your arms out in front of you. Raise them up high over your head. Way back. Feel the pull in your shoulders. Stretch higher. Now just let your arms drop back to your side. Okay, kitten, let's stretch again. Stretch your arms out in front of you. Raise them over your head. Pull them back, way back. Pull hard. Now let them drop quickly. Good. Notice how your shoulders feel more relaxed. This time let's have a great big stretch.

Try to touch the ceiling. Stretch your arms way out in front of you. Raise them way up high over your head. Push them way, way back. Notice the tension and pull in your arms and shoulders. Hold tight, now. Great. Let them drop very quickly and feel how good it is to be relaxed. It feels good and warm and lazy.

Jaw: You have a giant jawbreaker bubble gum in your mouth. It's very hard to chew. Bite down on it. Hard! Let your neck muscles help you. Now relax. Just let your jaw hang loose. Notice that how good it feels just to let your jaw drop. Okay, let's tackle that jawbreaker again now. Bite down. Hard! Try to squeeze it out between your teeth. That's good. You're really tearing that gum up. Now relax again. Just let your jaw drop off your face. It feels good just to let go and not have to fight that bubble gum. Okay, one more time. We're really going to tear it up this time. Bite down. Hard as you can. Harder. Oh, you're really working hard. Good. Now relax. Try to relax your whole body. You've beaten that bubble gum. Let yourself go as loose as you can.

Face and Nose: Here comes a pesky old fly. He has landed on your nose. Try to get him off without using your hands. That's right, wrinkle up your nose. Make as many wrinkles in your nose as you can. Scrunch your nose up real hard. Good. You've chased him away. Now you can relax your nose. Oops, here he comes back again. Right back in the middle of your nose. Wrinkle up your nose again. Shoo him off. Wrinkle it up hard. Hold it just as tight as you can. Okay, he flew away. You can relax your face. Notice that when you scrunch up your nose your cheeks and your mouth and your forehead and your eyes all help you, they get tight too. So when you relax your nose, your whole body relaxes too, and that feels good. Oh-oh. This time that old fly has come back, but this time he's on your forehead. Make lots of wrinkles. Try to catch him between all those wrinkles. Hold it tight, now. Okay, you can let go. He's gone for good. Now you can just relax. Let your face go smooth, no wrinkles anywhere. Your face feels nice and smooth and relaxed.

Stomach: Hey! Here comes a cute baby elephant. But he's not watching where he's going. He doesn't see you lying in the grass, and he's about to step on your stomach. Don't move. You don't have time to get out of the way. Just get ready for him. Make your stomach very hard. Tighten up your stomach muscles real tight. Hold it. It looks like he is going the other way. You can relax now. Let your stomach go soft. Let it be as relaxed as you can. That feels so much better. Oops, he's coming this way again. Get Ready. Tighten up your stomach. Real hard. If he steps on you when your stomach is hard, it won't hurt. Make your stomach into a rock. Okay, he's moving away again. You can relax now. Kind of settle down, get comfortable, and relax. Notice the difference between a tight stomach and a relaxed one. That's how we want to feel—nice and loose and relaxed. You won't believe this, but this time he's coming your way and no turning around. He's headed straight for you. Tighten up. Tighten hard. Here he comes. This is really it. You've got to hold on tight. He's stepping on you. He's stepped over you. Now he's gone for good. You can relax completely. You're safe. Everything is okay, and you can feel nice and relaxed.

This time imagine that you want to squeeze through a narrow fence and the boards have splinters on them. You'll have to make yourself very skinny if you're going to make it through. Suck your stomach in. Try to squeeze it up against your backbone. Try to be skinny as you can. You've got to be skinny now. Just relax and feel your stomach being warm and loose. Okay, let's try to get through that fence now. Squeeze up your stomach. Make it touch your backbone. Get it real small and tight. Get it as skinny as you can. Hold tight, now. You've got to squeeze through. You got through that narrow little fence and no splinters! You can relax now. Settle back and let your stomach come back out where it belongs. You can feel really good now. You've done fine.

Legs and Feet: Now pretend that you are standing barefoot in a big, fat mud puddle. Squish your toes down deep into the mud. Try to get your feet down to the bottom of the mud puddle. You'll probably need your legs to help you push. Push down, spread your toes apart, feel the mud squish up between your toes. Now step out of the mud puddle. Relax your feet. Let your toes go loose and feel how nice that it feels to be relaxed. Back into the mud puddle. Squish your toes down. Let your leg muscles help push your feet down. Push your feet. Hard. Try to squeeze that puddle dry. Okay. Come back out now. Relax your feet, relax your legs, relax your toes. It feels so good to be relaxed. No tenseness anywhere. You feel kind of warm and tingly.

Conclusion: Stay as relaxed as you can. Let your whole body go limp and feel all your muscles relaxed. In a few minutes I will ask you to open your eyes, and that will be the end of this practice session. As you go through the day, remember how good it feels to be relaxed. Sometimes you have to make yourself tighter before you can be relaxed, just as we did in these exercises. Practice these exercises everyday to get more and more relaxed. A good time to practice is at night, after you have gone to bed and the lights are out and you won't be disturbed. It will help you get to sleep. Then, when you are really a good relaxer, you can help yourself relax at bedtime. Just remember the elephant, or the jaw breaker, or the mud puddle, and you can do our exercises and nobody will know. Today is a good day, and you are ready to feel very relaxed. You've worked hard and it feels good to work hard. Very slowly, now, open your eyes and wiggle your muscles around a little. Very good. You've done a good job.

CHAPTER 4

Self-Invalidation

Self-invalidation is the tendency to invalidate or fail to recognize one's own emotion responses, thoughts, beliefs, and behaviors. The self-invalidating client usually will set unrealistically high standards and expectations for himself or herself. This may include intense shame, self-hate, and self-directed anger. Often this problem stems from invalidating environments.

An invalidating environment is one in which communication of private experiences is met by erratic, inappropriate, and extreme responses. In other words, the expression of private experiences is not validated; instead, it is often punished, and/or trivialized. The experience of painful emotions, as well as the factors that to the emotional person seem causally related to the emotional distress, are disregarded. The individual's interpretations of her own behavior, including the experience of the intents and motivations associated with behavior, are dismissed (Linehan, 1993, p.49).

THE CHILDHOOD ENVIRONMENT

Invalidating environments during childhood contribute to the development of emotion dysregulation; they also:

- fail to teach the child how to label and regulate arousal,
- how to tolerate emotional distress, and
- when to trust her own emotional responses as reflections of valid interpretations of events (Linehan, 1993, p. 42).

Extreme Reactions

"Emotional intensity" means that emotional reactions are extreme. Emotionally intense individuals are the dramatic people of the world. Partings may precipitate very intense and painful grief. What would cause slight embarrassment for another may cause deep humiliation; annoyance may turn to rage; shame may develop from slight guilt; apprehension may escalate to a panic attack or incapacitating terror.

Consequences of Invalidation

The consequences of invalidating environments are as follows. First, by failing to validate emotional expression, an invalidating environment does not teach the child to label private experiences, including emotions, in a manner normative in her larger social community for the same or similar experiences. Nor is the child taught to modulate emotional arousal. The child is told to control her emotions, rather than being taught exactly how to do that. It is a bit like telling a child with no legs to walk without providing artificial legs for her to walk on.

Catabolic State

Stress theory explains that the body tenses, muscles clench, breathing becomes shallow, the heart beats faster, the field of focus becomes narrow: the fight/flight response has been activated.

Biology Not Reason Rules

If this theory holds true, a child will find himself or herself reacting in an intense way but will not know why. In this intensity, the focus of the child will narrow, blocking out stimuli. Imagine sitting in a classroom and having this happen—the subject being taught will be shut out and the stressing event will occupy the child. On top of that, it will be hard for the child to resume normal functioning quickly.

Emotion Modulation

The research on emotional behavior suggests that emotion regulation requires practical strategies that "normal individuals" seem to learn. The individual must learn to experience and label the discrete emotions that are hard-wired into the neurophysiological, behavioral—expressive, and sensory—feeling systems.

"Normal" Individuals

Somewhere learn that there is a connection between feelings and thoughts and that thoughts influence their behavior. This is one area where Cognitive Behavior Therapy (CBT) comes into play with DBT.

CBT REVIEW

Albert Ellis, the founder of Rational Emotive Behavior Therapy, provides a quick review model for CBT.

With CBT, practitioners need at least use:

- Thought Records
- Schema Change Procedures
- Positive Data Logs
- Activity Scheduling

The Ellis A B C D E Model

A – Activating Event

B – Beliefs (Self-Talk)

Rational Beliefs: Thoughts that create socially acceptable feelings and actions

Irrational Beliefs: Thoughts that contain childish demandingness, critical evaluation of self or others, or problematic thinking

C – Consequences

Affect, Behavior, Cognitions

D – Disputing

Using Schema Change Methods

E – Effects of Disputing

Rational thinking

With Children and Adolescents

We have to determine whether they understand their own feelings and whether or not they can make the connection between thoughts and feelings. The following exercises will assist you in making that determination with very young children up through teenagers

LABELING EMOTIONS: WORK WITH YOUNG CHILDREN

Children Must Learn to Label Emotions

There are several exercises that help youths of various ages identify and label emotions.

Directions: Give a young child marking pens and paper with three evenly spaced boxes (so that writing can be fitted in above and below the pictures and ask young children to draw 3 different faces (Happy, Sad, Angry). Then start with the happy picture and ask the child what makes them feel happy (ask younger children when they feel happy).Write down what the child says around the picture.

Happy Face	Sad Face	Angry Face

WORKSHEET FOR IDENTIFYING FEELINGS

Directions: Create a collage. Obtain a poster board 24 inches by 36 inches. Look in magazines/newspapers and cut out words, phrases, and other pictures that reflect your feelings about anything you would like to discuss. Arrange the pictures and words/phrases and secure them on the poster board in any way you feel best expresses your feelings. When you have completed your collage, you and I will work together to answer the following questions:

1. Explain briefly the pictures you chose and which two have the greatest significance for you.

2. Explain the reasons for the words/phrases you chose.

3. Looking over the collage you've created, what does it say to you about your feelings?

4. Do the pictures bring back any of the following feelings? (Circle any that apply.)

Anger	Guilt	Disappointment	Regret
Hurt	Worry	Abandonment	Rejection
Happy	Fun	Fear	Joy
Love	Peace	Satisfaction	Empowerment

Other: _____

Explain: _____

_____

_____

_____

LETTER WRITING TO EXPRESS FEELINGS

Directions: Sometimes it is difficult to talk straight out to a counselor. I want you to write a letter to me discussing anything you might want to talk about. This can be a way to help identify and express your thoughts and feelings. This is especially true when you need to work through your feelings and understand your thinking about something. In this homework assignment, you are asked to write a letter to me about anything you want to help you identify and express your own feelings. You will give this letter to me at the beginning of our next session.

These are the steps you need to follow:

- First, find a quiet or relaxing place where you can write the letter. This will help you concentrate on writing down your thoughts and feelings without distractions. Perhaps you can write the letter in a quiet room in your house, at the library, or in a favorite outdoor place.

- Respond to the following questions designed to help you organize your thoughts and feelings before you begin to actually write the letter. You may find that some of these questions do not apply to you; therefore, leave those items blank. Space is also provided for you to express any additional thoughts or feelings that you may want to at this stage in the assignment. You can decide later as to whether you want to include these thoughts in your final letter.

1. What thoughts and feelings have you been experiencing?

2. What are some of the positive things in your life right now?

3. What are some of the hurts, problems, or disappointments in your life right now?

4. If something has not gone well for you, what, if anything, do you wish you could have said or done?

5. What mostly affects your present life?

6. Are you sorry about anything that has happened in your life? Describe.

7. Has your life changed recently? Describe.

8. What are some of the important events that have occurred in your life?

9. What do you think is the most important thing that we can work on together?

10. How do you feel about coming to counseling?

RECOGNIZING MY FEELINGS

(Adaptation of Bisignano & McElmurry, 1987)

Directions: This chart will help you recognize your feelings and help you understand the degree to which you experience each.

Check the appropriate box.

	Usually	Often	Sometimes	Seldom	Never
1. I feel happy					
2. I feel sad					
3. I feel lonely					
4. I feel accepted					
5. I feel bored					
6. I feel afraid					
7. I feel angry					
8. I feel peaceful					
9. I feel loved					
10. I feel hopeful					
11. I feel irritated					
12. I feel argumentative					
13. I feel like crying					
14. I feel like I don't care					
15. I feel like I can't sleep					
16. I feel disorganized					
17. I feel sick					
18. I feel stupid					
19. I feel like others are watching me					

FEELINGS CHECKLIST

(Adapted from Riethmayer, 1993)

Directions: In order to allow your feelings to help you know what you need, this week put a check by all of the feelings that you remember feelings that day. Remember, feelings are clues and signal about what's wrong or what we need. They are there to help you—if you learn to use them correctly. Begin to learn to name a feeling when you are having it.

Practice This Week With This Daily Checklist

Feeling	Mon.	Tues.	Wed.	Thurs.	Fri.	Sat.	Sun.
Anger							
Sad							
Guilty							
Lonely							
Embarrassed							
Happy							
Afraid							
Nervous							
Disappointed							
Hate							
Frustrated							
Disgusted							
Love							
Caring							
Sure							
Jealous							
Excited							
Bored							
Confused							
Numb							
Hurt							
Calm							
Safe							
Scared							
Playful							
Shy							
Really Sad							
Ashamed							
Worried							
Panicked							
Abandoned							

FEELING GAME

Directions: Tell the child, "Let's play a pretend game about feelings. You will take a turn pretending something happens to you. Then you show how you feel about it using your voice and your body. Watch me pretend a feeling and then guess what I am feeling."

<u>Counselor models</u>: spilling a pretend coke; saying, "Bummer!" and showing a feeling of disgust; and saying, "How do you think I feel?"

Role plays: Guide the client in acting out the role plays and showing how they would feel in the situation. If there are two roles have the child play the feeling role and you play the other role. If you are in a group, ask the group to guess the feeling.

- A car honks at you. (afraid)
- You are given a surprise gift. (surprised)
- You accidentally spill soup in the cafeteria. (disgusted)
- Someone jumps out at you. (surprised or afraid)
- You can't find anyone to watch TV with. (sad)
- You open the bag and find mold on bread. (disgusted)
- A friend tells you s/he likes you. (happy)
- You just started a new class and don't know anyone. (afraid, shy)

Do you notice that there are all kinds of feelings? I might have different kinds of feelings than you. For example, when a car honks, I might feel irritated at the person honking the horn or sorry for the driver who is upsetting himself. This has a lot to do with I tell myself about the situation. For example,

- A car honks at me. Instead of being afraid, I might tell myself, *"What is wrong with the driver of that car! He is stupid!"* and the feeling I would have is a feeling of being irritated.

  Or, I might tell myself, *"The poor guy behind me is making himself upset over nothing,"* and the feeling I would have would be feeling sorry for the driver.

- I am given a surprise gift. Instead of being surprised, I might tell myself, *"Oh no! It must be our anniversary and I forgot to get my husband a card!"* and my feeling would be one of dismay.

  Or, I might tell myself, *"It's my birthday and I like it that someone remembered,"* and my feeling would be one of happiness.

You accidentally spill soup in the cafeteria what do you tell yourself if you are disgusted?

_____

_____

_____

What could you tell yourself instead and what other feeling would you have?

_____

_____

_____

Sometimes you tell yourself that you are bad or worthless. Write down when that happened last.

_____

_____

_____

Now, write down something else you could tell yourself in that situation.

_____

_____

_____

Do you understand that you can make yourself feel bad and that you can change that feeling? Tell me about other situations where you make yourself feel bad and tell yourself that you are worthless, bad or stupid.

1. _____

2. _____

3. _____

Tell me what you can say to yourself to change this feeling:

1. _____

2. _____

3. _____

UNDERSTANDING SIMILAR AND DIFFERENT FEELINGS

Directions: Tell the child, "Let's play another game. We are going to stand face to face. We are going to pretend something happens to us and we will make a face to show how we feel."

Counselor and then client: Reacting to being served carrots at dinner.

Role play: Have the client go first and then as the counselor model a different feeling.

- A friend wants to show you her huge dog.
- You just found out your parents are going to have another baby.
- A friend rolled down a hill and wants you to join him.
- It's your turn to give a speech in class.
- You are given a big bowl of ice cream.
- You are given a new toy.
- Your uncle just bought your sister a new doll.
- It is your turn to jump in a mud puddle.
- You are given spinach at lunch.
- You are chosen to lead a game.

In each situation each of us had a different feeling. Why do you suppose that is true? (Correct answer because we tell ourselves different things about each event)

Sometimes when you feel down, you have telling yourself something that is not helpful.

When was the last time you felt down? What did you tell yourself? Instead of telling yourself that, what could you say to yourself instead? Let's write this down:

Situation: _____

_____

My thoughts: _____

_____

What I can say instead: _____

_____

_____

Who Is Responsible for Feelings?

Children can be taught that others are not responsible for their feelings and that are the ones who can control both what they think and how they feel. The exercise "Others Are Not Responsible for Our Feelings" is one exercise that will involve youths in a therapeutic educational session

The Thought Record

Date	Situation	Thoughts	Feelings	Actions

OTHERS ARE NOT RESPONSIBLE FOR OUR FEELINGS

Directions: Provide the client with a pen and a chart on paper. The chart should look like the one below. Note that young people can more easily identify feelings and then thoughts.

Situation	Feelings	Thoughts

Then begin a discussion.

Discuss what it means to be disappointed. Provide a self-disclosed example and write it out on the chart with the client watching. Example:

Situation	Feelings	Thoughts
I wanted cake for dessert and there was nothing for dessert.	I felt irritated.	I thought my husband (wife) should have made something for dessert.

Ask the youth to make a list of the last three times s/he was disappointed, to explain how s/he reacted to the disappointment (cried, yelled, argued, blamed, etc.), how s/he felt, and what s/he thought. Concentrate on the thoughts and feelings. Write the three situations on a chart; if possible have the youth write this himself or herself.

Situation	Feelings	Thoughts
Disappointment: 1:		
Disappointment: 2:		
Disappointment: 3:		

Ask the client to identify who they think is to blame for his or her unhappiness or disappointment in each situation.

Take the first situation and illustrate that unhappy feelings come from our thoughts. For example, if the client is disappointed that he or she was not able to sit by a friend at lunch, s/he would likely be thinking and saying to herself or himself something like:

"No one likes me."

"That no-good Fred. He should have left a spot for me."

"I am pretty mad right now."

Discuss the fact that not everyone would think and feel the way the client thinks and feels. For example, another student might think and say:

"It's too bad I didn't ask Fred to save me a seat."

"I need to tell Fred that I would like to sit next to him next time."

"I didn't get what I wanted so I will have to figure out what to do next time."

Ask the child to decide how s/he would have felt after saying the last things to herself or himself.

Go through all three situations the client has provided and have the child develop different statements and discuss the different feelings in relation to less critical, less demanding, and less childish (all elements of irrational thinking). This is also a good time to point out that sometimes our thoughts contain problematic thinking and this is a time to begin to dispute such thinking. Remember that problematic thinking includes forms of thinking like:

Shouldistic thinking—"People should treat me the way I want to be treated." "I should get what I want out of life with little or no hassle." "People should be . . ."

Musterbation—"I must be treated with respect and kindness." "I must do well in all of my endeavors."

Awfulizing—"It is awful and terrible that things aren't going my way." "This is so awful that things will never be better."

I-Can't-Stand-It-Itis—"You make me so mad that I can't stand it any more."

Wormhood—"You are such a worm for doing what you did that you should be severely blamed and punished." "I am so bad that I should be damned and I don't deserve anything from life."

You would ask the child who makes the statement, *"No one likes me"* to provide the evidence that no one likes him or her and you would dispute the thought by helping the child provide evidence that indeed someone does like him or her.

You would take the statement, *"That no-good Fred. He should have left a spot for me,"* and discuss the fact that no one always gets what s/he wants in life, and although it would have been nice if the student had been able to sit next to Fred, there is no rhyme, reason, or rule about who *should* get to do that.

You would take the statement, *"I'm pretty mad right now,"* and explain to the child that s/he is the one deciding to be mad and that other statements would make them feel differently.

INTENTIONS AND FEELINGS

People make mistakes or have accidents at some time or another. Tell the students that they are going to practice deciding when something is an accident and when something is done on purpose. For each of the following situations, have the student tell whether s/he thinks the action was an accident or done on purpose.

- Throwing a ball which hurts a kid's finger when she catches it. *(Accidental)*

- Pulling the chair away when someone starts to sit down in it, causing the person to fall down. *(On purpose)*
- Blowing a balloon up so big that it pops and makes a baby cry. *(Accidental, if it is the first time)*
- Hitting a friend because he hit you. *(On purpose)*
- Not looking as you turn around really fast, causing someone to spill juice on the floor. *(Accidental)*
- Swinging on a friend's swing set when the chain breaks. *(Accidental)*
- Pulling up the flowers in a neighbor's flower bed. *(On purpose)*
- Forgetting to return a phone call, causing her to feel hurt. *(Accidental)*
- Sticking your foot out in the aisle so that somebody trips. *(On purpose)*
- Lying on the grass looking for a 4 leaf clover when someone trips over you. *(Accidental)*

Role play: Have clients role-play the accidental situations above, this time making an apology and offering help.)

<u>Counselor models</u>: pretending to throw a ball which hurts a student's fingers and saying, *"I'm sorry. It was an accident. What can I do to help?"*

AFTER LEARNING TO IDENTIFY FEELINGS

Children and adolescents will have taken the first step in training. Much more teaching needs to occur. Remember that students and clients with emotional dysregulation feel things intensely and are easily aroused and activated. Once an intense emotion is activated, the individual must be able to inhibit or interfere with the activation of mood-congruent afterimages, afterthoughts, after-appraisals, after-expectations, and after-actions. They do not know how to do this and must be taught.

CHAPTER 5

Unrelenting Crises & Active Passivity

Unrelenting crises involve patterns of frequent, stressful, negative environmental events, disruptions, and roadblocks—some caused by the individual's dysfunctional lifestyle others by an inadequate social milieu, and many by fate or chance.

Active passivity is defined as the tendency to passive interpersonal problem-solving style, involving failure to engage actively in solving of own life problems, often together with active attempts to solicit problem solving from others in the environment and as a result of learned helplessness and hopelessness.

Many young people come to counselors in crisis. Linehan has discussed rules about crises (Linehan, 1995). The first rule is that if you can solve a crisis, solve it but if you cannot solve it, survive it. Often young people want a therapist to solve their problems for them. To really mix a parable, problem solving has to be considered this way. If a person comes to your house to eat because they are hungry, you can fix them a fish dinner and take care of their hunger for part of one day. However, if you take that person to a river bank, provide them with a fishing pole, teach them how to bait a hook, land, fillet, and cook a fish, you have provided that person with a set of skills he or she can use to solve the hunger problem.

MODULATION ACTIVITIES

John Gottman and Lynn Katz (1990) have outlined four emotion modulation activities or abilities. These include the abilities to (1) inhibit inappropriate behavior related to strong negative or positive affect, (2) self-regulate physiological arousal associated with affect, (3) refocus attention in the presence of strong affect, and (4) organize one self for coordinated action in the service of an external, non-mood-dependent goal.

Inhibit Inappropriate Behavior

You will need to teach impulse control. For children this will involve teaching problem solving strategies.

The Steps of Problem Solving

You must ask and answer the following questions:

1. What is the problem?

2. What are some solutions?

3. For each solution ask:

    a. Can you do this safely?

    b. How might people feel?

    c. Is it fair?

    d. Will it work?

4. Chose a solution and use it.

5. Is it working? If not, what can I do now?

LEARNING SELF-REGULATION: CHOOSING SOLUTION ROLE PLAYS

The counselor will have the client practice brainstorming solutions by writing down some solutions to the problem presented. S/he will direct the client: *I am going to give you a problem situation and you will write out some solutions.*

The counselor models by saying "The problem is dad yells at you all of the time. If dad is yelling that must mean there is some type of problem. First we define the problem, and then we write down some solutions. First we can talk to dad to see why he might be yelling. Let's say that he is yelling because he wanted you to put away dinner dishes and you did not want to put your dish in the sink. Our first solution might be to ask a sister to put the dish into the sink for us. We ask our four questions about having sister do the work. If we answer negatively to any of the questions, then we need to choose another solution. Next we might decide to ask dad to put the dishes in the sink. We ask our four questions, but if we answer any oft hem them in a negative manner, we must choose another solution. Finally, we decide that we should put the dishes in the sink and if we can answer all questions in a positive way, that is the solution we need to try."

Client Role Plays: The client should repeat the problem as in the model role play and then ask and answer *"What are some solutions?"* and write them down. Then we ask all four questions about each solution to see if that is the best solution with positive answers.)

- Your sister wears your shirt without asking you first.
- Your brother broke your favorite toy.
- You don't want to go to church on Sunday morning.
- You don't like what your mother has fixed for dinner.
- Your brother turns to TV to a another show when you were in the middle of watching a program.

LEARNING SELF-REGULATION: PRACTICE PROBLEM SOLVING

The counselor will set up role plays in which clients use the problem-solving steps. The model is *"What is the problem? What are some solutions? Asking and answering the four evaluation questions for each solution. Choosing and trying a solution.*

Client role plays:

- Your friend has cookies in his lunch and you would like some but he does not usually share.

- Your mother has asked you to go shopping with her but you don't want to go.

- You have been asked to clean your room but you don't want to.

- Your homework is due tomorrow but you are tired.

- You want a new toy but your mother tells you that she does not have enough money to buy it right now.

- You want to go fishing with your dad but he is taking his buddies and no kids along for this trip.

- You want to sit in the front seat but your sister called "shotgun" first.

To Teach Self-Regulation

Find out where a student or client is having difficulty in school or life. Use those examples to teach what the child can do to handle the difficulty.

Learning Responsibility for Actions

In our society, it is much easier to blame others for life's problems than it is to accept responsibility for our own actions. Part of self-regulation is learning that sometimes we do things wrong or that we make mistakes. The self-regulating individual takes responsibility for his or her mistakes. The next slides endeavor to teach this skill.

LEARNING SELF-REGULATION: APOLOGIZING

The counselor will say, "In today's lesson you will learn how to take *responsibility* for your actions. Juan is in the library. He just picked up the librarian's coffee favorite cup and *accidentally dropped* it. The favorite cup broke. Nobody saw Juan break the favorite cup. He feels like walking away from it. Let's use the problem-solving steps to help solve Juan's problem."

1. What is the problem? (Juan accidentally broke the librarian's coffee favorite cup.)

2. What might happen if Juan walks away from it and pretends he knows nothing about what happened? (Both he and the librarian might feel bad.)

3. What could Juan do instead? (Apologize to the librarian; offer to get her another favorite cup; blame it on somebody else.)

4. What might happen if . . . ?

5. Juan chooses to tell the librarian what happened and *apologize.* By doing this he is taking *responsibility for* his actions.

6. When should he apologize? (As soon as possible.) An apology means not just saying you're sorry, but showing you're sorry by offering to make things better.

7. How could Juan make things better? (By gluing the broken favorite cup or getting her another favorite cup.)

8. Why do we make apologies? (To show we care about other people.)

9. What could Juan do if he apologizes to the librarian, but she gets mad at him anyway? (Keep a good attitude and repeat the apology.)

Let's write down steps for apologizing. What is the first thing Juan should do?

1. Say what happened.

2. Say you're sorry.

3. Offer to make things better.

For Adolescents There Are Other Problem Solving Strategies

CAUSE & EFFECT WORKSHEET—IDENTIFYING CAUSES OF PROBLEMS

Directions: This Cause & Effect Worksheets help you to think through causes of a problem thoroughly. Their major benefit is that they push you to consider all possible causes of the problem, rather than just the ones that are most obvious.

Follow these steps to solve a problem:

1. Identify the problem

Write down the exact problem you face in detail. Where appropriate identify who is involved, what the problem is, and when and where it occurs.

Those involved are: _____

_____

_____

The exact problem is: _____

_____

_____

It happens when: _____

_____ at _____

_____

2. Work out the major factors involved

Next identify the factors that may contribute to the problem. Try to draw out as many possible factors as possible.

The things that contribute to the problem are: _____

_____

_____

_____

_____

3. Identify possible causes

For each of the factors you considered in stage 2, brainstorm possible causes of the problem that may be related to the factor.

Causes of the problem are: _____

_____

_____

_____

4. Analyze your diagram

Possible solutions to the problem include: _____

_____

_____

_____

What else can be taught?

CHAPTER 6

Inhibited Grieving

Inhibited grieving is the tendency to inhibit and over control negative emotional responses, especially those associated with grief and loss, including sadness, anger, guilt, shame, anxiety, and panic.

GRIEF

Researchers like Rando (1984) have indicated that there are three basic tasks of grief that one must work through in relation to a significant loss in one's life. The first task has been called emancipation from bondage and relates to Freud's concept of decathexis. *Mourning has a quite precise psychical task to perform; Its function is to detach the survivors' memories and hopes from the dead (Freud, 1913, p.65).*

Decathexis

When humans are involved with one another, they invest emotional energy into that person. A therapist would need to work with a youth to determine all the ties that bind him or her to the lost person and help the child work through each strong tie and hope to release that emotional energy.

Second and Third Steps of Grief

The second step in grief work is to help the youth to live in the world in which the deceased or divorced person is missing—teaching them do the things that person used to do for them. The third step of grief work involves forging new relationships—with the deceased or missing person, with friends and others.

Not Inhibiting Grief

In today's society, children and adolescents experience too much loss. Our discussion here will examine only losses related to death and separation and specific activities will be proposed to help children learn to grieve.

Children who are coming to terms with the death of a family member, friend, or even a pet, experience very real grief which may be expressed through behavior problems as well as depressed mood. Losses apply in cases of separation from parents or other significant people in the child's life. Just like adults, children can become stuck in their grief, and we have found these exercises usually help them to move forward. They will assist the child to accept his loss, have good memories and carry on with his life.

To Assess Grief in Different Ages

<u>*How Do We Assess the Loss?*</u>

QUESTIONNAIRE FOR GRIEVER'S PROFILE CHILDREN AND TEENS DEALING WITH A LOSS DUE TO DEATH

Counselor's Name: _____ **Date:** _____

Questions are to be asked by the counselor to the child. The counselor will write down the verbal responses and non-verbal responses of the child. Words written in italics are for the counselor only.

This questionnaire could take more than one counseling session to fill out depending on the client.

Client's Name: _____

Age: _____ **Grade in School:** _____ **Ethnicity:** _____

(Needed for estimating maturity level and cognition level of student and cultural background)

Referred By: _____

Reason for Referral: _____

_____

_____

PSYCHOLOGICAL FACTORS INFLUENCING THE GRIEF REACTION:

1. Please begin by telling me who you have lost to death. _____

_____

_____

2. What does losing this person mean to you personally & how has it affected you personally? _____

_____

_____

3. On a scale of 1-10, with 1 being the least and 10 being the absolute most, circle the number that represents how close you were to the individual?

   1　2　3　4　5　6　7　8　9　10

4. When someone has a 'role' in a family, what we are saying is what their job or position is in the family. For example a dad might be the main one who works and brings home money, takes kids fishing and to Boy Scouts while mom also works, cleans the house, cooks and helps kids with homework, Girl Scouts etc.

   Thinking about the person you have lost in your family, how would you describe his/her 'role' in your family? _____

   _____

   _____

5. Since this person has died, who has taken on the 'roles' of that person in your family and what 'roles' have they taken on? Be sure to include yourself in your answer. _____

   _____

   _____

6. In the past when you have experienced some kind of loss, like losing a pet or your best friend having to move away, what have you done to help you get over that loss or make the loss less painful?*(Other examples may be inserted depending on the client's past experiences) (Looking for previous coping behaviors and personality in answer.)* _____

   _____

   _____

7. As the counselor, what level of maturity and intelligence would you estimate is the client with whom you are working? _____

   _____

   _____

8. When someone says the word 'death' or 'dead' to you, what does that mean to you or what do you envision or imagine? *(Counselor learning to what degree the client cognitively understands the meaning and implications of death)* _____

   _____

   _____

9. Have you ever experienced losing someone to death? If yes, do you remember when? How old were you? How close were you to that person?

    _____

    _____

    _____

10. What has your family and/or people you are around taught you about death and how to react to it in your growing up years? What have you observed is the way they deal with death? *(Counselor is learning the social, cultural, ethnic and religious/philosophical background)* _____

    _____

    _____

11. How have your parents and/or other adults and friends taught you about how men and boys are supposed to react when they are sad or hurt? How have your parents and/or other adults and friends taught you about how women and girls are supposed to react when they are sad?_____

    _____

    _____

12. Thinking now about the person you have lost to death, please describe for me in as much detail as you want what your relationship was with this person.

    _____

    _____

    _____

13. Could you tell me about how old this person was when he/she died? _____

14. Since some time has passed since this person *(say the person's name if client is comfortable with it)* has died, do you think about wishing you could have said something to *(name of deceased)* before he/she died? If so, what do you wish you could have said? _____

    _____

    _____

15. Do you believe that *(name of deceased)* lived a full life and that he/she was able to do all the things that he/she wanted or needed to do in life? Please explain.

_____

_____

_____

16. I know how painful this must be and I am truly sorry for this, but in order to help me be to able to help you, I need to understand more about the way *(name of deceased)* died. Could you tell me in your own words what you can about how he/she died? Take as much time as you need _____

_____

_____

17. *(Counselor possibly now has information about whether this was a sudden death or an illness related death and should know if the illness was short or long term. With this information, **gently** find out how the client feels about the timeline of the death.)*

What are your feelings about the suddenness or length of illness of *(name of deceased's)* that lead to his/her death? *(Get a feel for your client before asking this and be as gentle as possible, putting question in your own words if possible.)* _____

_____

_____

18. Do you feel that *(name of deceased's)* death could have been prevented or stopped? If so, could you please explain to me why you feel this way? If not, could you please explain to me why you feel this way? _____

_____

_____

19. **(Only** *if the client has **not** already divulged information about suddenness or length of illness, then ask this next question.)*

Was *(name of deceased's)* death sudden or was it the result of an illness. If it was an illness, could you tell me about how long he/she was sick? _____

_____

_____

20. Have you experienced any other losses as a result of the death? If so, can you explain what they are? _____

_____

_____

Social Factors Influencing the Grief Reaction:

21. Who do you have in your family or in you circle of friends that you can confide in and feel supported? _____

_____

_____

22. Could you describe for me what religion you are or where you go to church if you and your family go? _____

_____

_____

23. Was there a funeral for (*name of deceased*) and if so, did you get to attend?

_____

_____

Physiological Factors Influencing Grief Reaction:

24. Are you on any kind of medication and if so for what? _____

_____

_____

25. What do you usually eat in a normal day? _____

_____

_____

26. Approximately how many hours sleep do you get at night? (*If the client can't tell number of hours, ask what time do they normally go to bed and get up.*)

_____

_____

27. How much exercise do you get in a day? _____

_____

28. What kind of exercise do you usually do? _____

_____

The following questionnaire may be used with the adult population.

Name: _____ **Date:** _____

Birth date: _____ **Sex:** ___ Male ___ Female

Relationship to the deceased: _____

1. What are your past experiences with loss and death?

2. What is the nature of the loss and what does it mean to you?

3. Tell some qualities of the relationship you had with the person whom you have lost.

4. How fulfilled was the person's life?

5. What have you done to cope with your loss?

6. Is there any unfinished business left with the deceased person?

7. Do you have a support system which is accepting of you and that can assist you in coping with your grief?

8. Please list members or groups of your support system.

9. What is your religious preference?

10. What is your idea of a funerary ritual?

11. Do you have a history of mental illness?

12. Are you currently taking any medication?

13. Have you experienced a change in appetite or weight? If yes, explain.

14. What do you currently do for exercise?

15. Are you in overall good physical health? If your answer is no, please list source of illness.

GRIEF AND LOSS QUESTIONNAIRE FOR TEENS

Tell me about what has happened.

What was your relationship with _____?

Tell me about it.

Did you spend a lot of time with _____?

Describe your typical day.

Describe a typical day with _____. *If the answer to the previous question doesn't include the deceased.*

What will be different now?

Who will do the things _____ used to do?

Will you have new jobs or responsibilities now?

Have you ever lost someone or something important before?

Tell me about it. *(Watch for avoidance)*

How did you feel?

How did you deal with _____? *(If enough info is not revealed, then I would ask the next question.)*

Can you tell me about another bad thing that has happened to you?

How did you feel?

Did anything happen because you felt _____?

Did you try to forget about _____?

Did you try to keep busy?

Did you want to talk about _____ all the time or want to be around people (not alone) more?

Did you make or try to make any major decisions just after _____?

Tell me about _____. *(The deceased)*

How did _____ treat you?

How do you feel about _____'s life?

Do you feel that _____ lived a fulfilled life?

Did anything positive or significant happen to _____ just before death?

How did it happen?

Where did it happen?

Do you know why it happened?

What else do you know about it?

Is there anything you want to know or do not want to know about it?

Do you feel as if it could have been prevented?

Do you feel responsible in any way?

Was the death sudden or was it expected due to an illness?

How long have you known? More than 6 months?

Did you have any additional responsibilities or will you have any now?

Did the illness ever go into remission? How many times? *(Repeated remission could cause emotional stress or guilt if he/she wanted loved one to die to relieve stress and responsibility.)*

Were you more involved or less involved with _____ before his/her death?

Was there time to finish business? to say good-bye, I love you, I'm sorry, to resolve issues never addressed or any past conflicts?

What else do you feel that you've lost besides _____? *(House, income, participation in extra curricular activities.)*

How do you see the future without _____?

How has the make-up of your family and its responsibilities changed?

Do you play a more important role in your family now? (work to earn money, male becoming head of family)

How do you feel about yourself?

Do you feel worthless or useless? How often?

Do you feel as though you let those you care about down?

How do you feel when you make a mistake?

Do you ask other people's opinions before making decisions?

Does it bother you if someone doesn't like you?

Have you ever been depressed before?

Are there any other conflicts in your life?

Do you have any other stresses unrelated to death, such as trouble with grades, relationships, money?

Will there be any of these stressors now?

Will you be able to resume with your normal ways of living?

Tell me about your family.

Do you feel like they are compassionate and supportive?

Do they offer you encouragement and are nonjudgmental?

Do they expect a lot from you? *(Watch for signs of inappropriate expectations from others and self isolation.)*

How are deaths in your family usually handled?

BEST MEMORY PICTURE—AGE: 3 YEARS & UP

Aim: To assist the progression of grief through drawing/artwork.

Materials: Paper and pencils, marking pens, paint, crayons, or pictures and glue/tape.

Method: Ask the child what his best memory is of the person/pet who has died. Work out together how you could recreate this memory pictorially, and then do it, with the child being involved as much as possible. During the task or afterwards, discuss the picture to draw out the child's memory, using questions such as the following:

- Why is it the best memory?
- What else does it make you think about?
- What will you do with the picture?
- What would the person/pet think of the picture?
- What will other people think of the picture (does it matter)?

Adolescents

Include in the discussion any other topics that may arise from the picture, such as, what happens when someone dies. Reinforce that although the person has died, the memories have not gone.

Variation: Many Memories

This can be used for not just the best memory, but as a collection of memories. This activity can be done with more than one person, for example, the family, so long as ground rules about respecting other people's memories are firmly established, and it is recognized that different people remember things in different ways.

REMEMBER BOOK—AGE: 3 YEARS AND UP

Aim: To assist the progression of grief through working on the memory of times and events associated with the person/pet who has died.

Materials: Exercise book or special folder with pages, paper, and marking pens.

Method: Ask the child if she would like to write a special book about the person/pet who has died. First, on a loose sheet of paper, write down all the memories that the child has of the deceased. They don't have to be all good, although for this purpose, most of the memories are likely to be good, and the child probably wants to dwell on those. Depending on the child's age, you may want to write a little description of the person who has died, along with his favorite foods, baseball team, and so on, and you may write about what the child had in common with him, or what they didn't have in common. Then work out together which order these facts/memories should go in they can be in chronological order, or sorted according to topic, or whatever suits the child. Write the book together, with the child doing as much on her own as possible (ensuring that the product is readable). She may like to include photos or illustrations, old tickets of places attended together, or other keepsakes. At the end of the book, include the fact that although the person/pet has died, memories can be kept alive.

A Book About . . .

This style of book writing can also be used to help in the grief associated with abuse, in that the child can benefit from writing about the good and the bad in someone whom she loved, but who abused her. Make sure the activity ends on a positive survivor note.

MEMORY CANDLE—AGE: 7 YEARS AND UP

Aim: To have a specific time when the child remembers the person who has died and has the opportunity to talk about her and grieve.

Materials: A candle which will burn for around 15 minutes. Have spare candles ready in case the child needs longer for the task. If you only have a large candle, make marks on it to indicate when it will be blown out.

Method: Introduce the task by talking about how people sometimes light candles in churches to remember someone who has died. Explain that when you light the candle, the child will be able to watch **it** burn, and it will be a special time to remember the person for whom the child is grieving. Light the candle and encourage the child to talk. He may avoid eye contact with you by concentrating on the candle. Have some questions handy to help the child if he becomes anxious, but do not be afraid of silence if the child appears to be able to cope with this. Ask the questions in a quiet, calm manner to aid the child's confidence and concentration. Some suitable questions might be:

> What color was her hair?
>
> Can you remember anywhere you went together?
>
> What is your best memory?
>
> Did she ever tell you a joke?
>
> Did she like animals?

If the child starts to cry, tell him that it is all right to be upset.

If the child becomes very anxious, uptight, or uncomfortable, ask if he would like the candle blown out, and if he says yes, extinguish it immediately. However, explain to the child that lots of people feel worried when they think about people who have died, but it is all right to think of them. Also tell the child how some people, even children, feel guilty when people die, even though it wasn't their fault and there was nothing they could have done.

As you end the activity, bring the child back to his life and encourage him to tell you about something he is looking forward to. However, he may need a cuddle and a hug from a caregiver before he is ready to leave the subject.

Often our clients will have difficulty gaining a realistic comprehension of and expectations for grief and mourning. This process may take many forms, however one of the more drastic areas is the client's inability to move forward with their life after the death of the loved one. Often clients will allow irrational thoughts, expectations, and faulty comprehension of the facts surrounding the death of a loved one to not only have a negative impact on the mourning process but also on their daily functioning. The following is a list of three interventions that can be used with client's having a difficult time adapting to a realistic view of life during the grief and mourning process.

LINKING OBJECTS

Aim: Use "linking objects" to assist the client in adapting to their new life without forgetting the old.

Method: In the mourning process "linking objects" are possessions of the deceased that have a special attachment to the client. They may be objects large or small that the client believes has a direct link to the loved one who has passed away. Such objects may be as small as a set of tools or baseball cards or as large as a car or a piece of real estate. In either case the client may have a difficult time disposing of the object because of the emotional linkage between the item and the deceased.

When counseling clients holding onto "linking objects" it is important to take the following steps:

1. Have the client identify what linking objects are now in their possession.

2. Ask the client why they link that object to the deceased.

3. Find out the direct relationship they may have with a linking object. For example if the object is a ten year old daughter's teddy bear, the client may sleep with the stuffed animal, however an older widow may keep her husband's power tools knowing she will never use them.

4. As the client begins to develop new relationships during the grieving process have them reevaluate steps one through three and identify if the objects still have the same power as they did before.

5. When the client begins to move past the stage of needing direct linking objects encourage the client to sell or dispose of any linking objects that are not needed for their everyday life.

THE FIVE R'S ADAPTED FROM RANDO, 1984

Using "The Five R's" process to assist clients in gaining a more realistic view of grieving.

Step One: RECOGNIZE. Train the client to identify not only when negative thoughts may occur, but also what those thoughts are. This can be done during the counseling process, for example a client may say, "I will never be able to go on without my wife." This would be an opportunity to point out to the client that they have expressed a negative thought and that they should be aware of such thoughts in the future.

Step Two: REFUSE: When the client can properly identify a negative thought they need to develop a ritual to refuse the negative thought when it occurs. Often one of the easiest techniques is for the client to wear a rubber band around their wrist and anytime they have a negative thought snap the band as a reminder that they need to refuse such thoughts.

Step Three: RELAX: When the client is relaxed they can better process and stop any negative thoughts that may occur. In this case the counselor may want to teach the client to use relaxing breathing techniques such as the one found at this website: http://www.pe2000.com/anx-breathe.htm

Step Four: REFRAME: The fourth step in the Negative Thought Stopping procedure serves to complete a mental shift toward images and thoughts that are consistent with a successful mourning process. Work with the clients to replace their negative thoughts with a positive image or thought. For example, "I AM in control of my thoughts and actions, I can choose to respond and think the way I want to." "I've been here before and done this before, so I know I can do it again."

Step Five: RESUME: Assist the client in using these techniques to continue their daily life with a sense of confidence and control. Continue to encourage the client that the degree of effort they apply to the challenges that you face on an ongoing basis during the grieving process is totally, 100% within their control. Also they can take comfort in the fact that during this difficult and trying time, it is one of the few things that is, in fact, fully within their control.

MYTHS AND STEREOTYPES

Aim: Assist the client in identifying their own myths and stereotypes about mourning and loss. Often our clients have a difficult time during the mourning process because they believe that there is a certain way that people of their gender, socio-economic or cultural background should grieve loved ones. Early in the counseling process it is important to go over the following list with our clients and learn about their views surrounding death and grieving while helping them correct any myths that could affect the mourning process:

Common Myths about Death and Grieving

Ask the client to answer **yes** if they believe each statement and **no** if they do not:

- All losses are the same.
- All bereaved people grieve in the same way.
- You will be the same after the death as before your loved one died.
- You will have no relationship with you loved one after the death.

Myths about the Timing of Grief:

It takes two months to get over your grief.

Grief always declines over time in a steadily decreasing fashion.

The intensity and length of your grief are testimony to your love for the person, pet or thing lost.

When grief is resolved, it never comes up again.

Myths about Avoiding the Pain of Grief:

If is better to put painful things out of your mind.

Once a loved one has died it is best to put him or her in the past and to go on with your life.

You should not think about the deceased at anniversaries or holidays because it will make you feel sad.

Myths about the Feelings of Grief:

Bereaved people need only to express their feelings and they will resolve their grief.

Expressing feelings that are intense is the sam as losing control.

There is no reason to be angry at people who tried to do their best for your loved one.

You should feel only sadness that your loved one has died.

Myths about the Physical Symptoms of Grief:

Grief will affect you psychologically, but in no other way.

Only sick individuals have physical problems in grief.

Myths about Support for Grief:

If is not important for you to have social support in your grief.

There is something wrong if you do not always feel close to your friends and family, since you should be happy that they are still alive.

It is better to tell bereaved people to "Be brave" and "Keep a stiff upper lip" because then they will not have to experience as much pain.

Rituals and funerals are unimportant in helping us deal with life and death in contemporary America.

References:

http://www.kilcrease.com/blog/2006/07/06/mourning-linking-objects.html

http://www.articlesalley.com/article.detail.php/30568/78/Success/
Self-Improvement/9/The_Five_R's_-_A_Negative_Thought_Stopping_Procedure

http://www.journeyofhearts.org/kirstimd/myths.htm

REPLENISHING SELF

Aim: To move a client out and about after a loss.

Methods: The therapist and client will discuss activities and things that they would like to do. The therapist and client will discuss what it would take for the client to participate in these activities. The therapist will give the client a homework assignment that would encourage the client to think about goals for the future, things that would help him to feel good about himself, activities that he would enjoy doing, and the steps that he would need to take to complete these tasks. The therapist and client will discuss the homework assignment in detail during the next therapy session. The therapist will encourage the client and give the client praise for completing the assignment. The therapist will also encourage to client to follow through with the goals.

The therapist will encourage the client to start to make goals and decisions about the future. The therapist will encourage the client to reinvest and move forward. The therapist will suggest that the client use an activity schedule that will let the client schedule activities of interest. The therapist will encourage and reward independence when activities are completed. The therapist will work with the client on scheduling activities that are pleasurable for the client in hopes of the activity having a positive effect on their mood and decrease feelings of helplessness.

Be specific and concrete with young people: Where, when, with whom, and for how long? Vagueness is death to activity scheduling. It is important to be concrete and specific when you make an activity plan. Specify exactly what activity will be carried out, where, when, with whom, how, for how long, and so on. For example, the client might agree to spend 15 minutes filing papers on her desk immediately after returning home after the therapy session. It is a good idea to use the Activity Schedule form to write down the plan that you and your client agree on; if possible, keep a copy and send one home with your client. Ask your client to bring the Activity Schedule to the next therapy session to review how successful he or she was at completing the planned activities.

Plan ahead for potential obstacles. Work with your client to try to anticipate and make a plan to handle obstacles and problems that might arise.

Often the therapist can anticipate obstacles that the client cannot. The therapist can point these out and work in the session to solve problems and overcome obstacles before they arise outside of the session and block the client from moving forward. For example, the client may set a plan to go to the movies with a friend. However, if none of his friends are reach-able by phone or have time to go out, the plan will fail. To address this obstacle, the therapist can suggest that the client make a plan to call a friend and to go to the movies alone if his friend is not available; this plan is much more likely to succeed. Sometimes, the client's view that activity scheduling is too trivial or simplistic is an obstacle. Cognitive restructuring may be helpful to overcome this problem. The client may insist that he or she has an alternative approach to the problem that is more likely to succeed. To address this, the therapist can suggest a behavioral experiment to test the client's hypothesis. The therapist can work with the client to try the client's intervention for a week, with the agreement that if this is not successful, the client will try activity scheduling.

ACTIVITY SCHEDULE

Time	Mon.	Tues.	Wed.	Thurs.	Fri.	Sat.	Sun.
7:00 am							
8:00 am							
9:00 am							
10:00 am							
11:00 am							
12:00 pm							
1:00 pm							
2:00 pm							
3:00 pm							
4:00 pm							
5:00 pm							
6:00 pm							
Evening							

The therapist and client will discuss the schedule and activities when they are accomplished. The therapist will give praise and encouragement for activities completed

STRESS REDUCING TIPS

*http://www.mckinley.uiuc.edu/Handouts/stress_reducing_tips.html_*

Aim: The therapist will work with the client on stress reducing techniques that will help the client through difficult times.

Slow-Down Techniques

10-SECOND BREATHING

In an acute situation, when your mind or body is racing out of control, slow down your breathing to a 10-second cycle, 6 breaths a minute. Find a clock or watch with a second hand and inhale for 5 seconds (odd number on clock face) then exhale for 5 seconds (even number). Keep it up for 2-5 minutes, or until your pace slows down.

60-SECOND BREAK

Close your eyes and take a deep breath. Visualize yourself lounging on a sunny beach, watching the sunset or relaxing in the shower or sauna.

5-MINUTE VACATION

Close your eyes and take a few deep breaths. Then visualize a favorite place or activity. Let your imagination carry you away to a special spot that's refreshing and relaxing.

CHEST MASSAGE

Relax your chest muscles and open up your breathing with a vigorous massage along the midline and across the chest below your collarbone.

BOTHER LIST

Write down a list of all the worries, pressures and concerns that are crowding your mind and clamoring for attention. Then burn the list or tuck it in your wallet for later attention.

PEACEFUL FOCUS

Focus on something pleasant and beautiful in your immediate environment (a blade of grass, a painting, a color). Concentrate on the beauty you see and breathe it in. Allow that beauty to slow you down.

Gear-Up Techniques

STRETCH AND MOVE

Stand up and stretch. Arch your back and stretch your arms and fingers out to the side. Hold that posture for awhile and then let go. Now move your body all around to get the blood pumping. Clap your hands. Jump up and down. MOVE!

EXHILARATION BREAK

Imagine yourself somewhere exciting, exhilarating or awe-inspiring (e.g., standing on a cliff above the ocean, performing for a large audience, cheering at an exciting football game, crossing the finish line at a race, laughing uproariously with friends, peering over the rim of the Grand Canyon, giving birth or watching birth). Let the vividness of that vision charge your batteries.

PEP TALK

Give yourself a pep talk. Use your best persuasive powers to motivate, encourage, cajole, support, cheer, challenge yourself. Ask somebody else to join in!

STIRRING MUSIC

Turn on some lively music like a march or a mazurka. Start moving. Dance. Bounce. March. Sing along. Get involved. Let the music pump you up and pull you along.

BODY BRACER

Gently pat or tap all over your body in an energizing rhythm. Keep it up until you tingle all over and are charged up.

EXERCISE

Vigorous exercise of any kind is a sure-fire way to get geared up. Add a creative twist for some extra punch.

Loosen-Up Techniques

PRETZEL

Imagine that your body is all tied up in knots and only you know how to untie them. Beginning with your toes and gradually moving up the body, tense and relax each set of muscles. Visualize that you are tightening the knots as you tense the muscles and picture yourself undoing the knots as you relax the muscles and let go.

BREATHE INTO TENSION

Close your eyes and take a deep breath. As you become aware of any points of tension, "breathe into" that spot, allowing the breath to bring calm to the area and carry away tension as you exhale.

SELF-MASSAGE

Reach across your body and massage the muscles of your neck and shoulder with long, firm strokes. Knead any especially tight areas with firm, circular or back and forth motions. Then repeat the process on the other side. With both hands massage the base of your skull with firm, circular strokes. Continue over the scalp and face, stopping to give special attention wherever you notice tension. Don't forget the jaw!

SHAKE A LEG

Stand up and shake an arm, a leg, the other arm, the other leg, your whole body. Then take a deep breath and let yourself go.

DEALING WITH ANGER

Aim: To help clients experience and express angry reactions.

"All Feelings Are Okay—It's What You Do With Them That Counts" activity book. This activity book allows the client to express what they are feeling and gives suggestions of how to effectively deal with those feelings. The activity book will help the client to better deal with their anger (All Feelings, 2007).

Utilize *"Face It!"* card game. Lots of times, anger comes from other feelings of abandonment, loss, grief, etc. This card game allows the client to face their feelings. The game deals with a plethora of feelings and how those feelings are dealt with at different stages in life such as childhood, adolescence, and adulthood. The client will not only face their feelings, but also face the same feelings during different times in their life (Face It, 2007).

SAYING GOODBYE

Aim: To teach the client to let go and cope.

Methods: The counselor and client will watch the video *Sometimes You Have to Say Goodbye.* In this video, the client will view three other children who are experiencing a loss. One has a friend that is moving away, another child lost their cat, and the other lost their grandfather. After viewing the video, the counselor and client will discuss how the different characters in the video dealt with their grief and how their coping strategies are different from the clients. Counselor/client will also discuss what coping strategies the client thought worked and which didn't and why. This will better help the client see that there is nothing wrong with the way they are grieving and help the counselor to let the client grieve (Sometimes, 2007).

The counselor will encourage the client to experience their feelings. The client will express one feeling per session that they are experiencing. For example, anger. The counselor will allow the client to look angry, act angry, and put words to their anger. This will help the client and counselor to work through the feeling during the session. The counselor and client will discuss the feeling and what is causing the feeling. If the client is finding it hard to use words to express this feeling and what is causing it, art therapy can be utilized.

Utilize "The Goodbye Game". This game will help the client to find closure about his/her perception and their understanding of the death of this loved one. The game outlines the five stages of grief and helps to break up myths of false understandings about death. The client will come out of the game with understanding about the concepts of death and grieving. The counselor and client will discuss what was learned from the game (Goodbye, 2007).

The counselor and client will read *Don't Despair on Thursday* by Adolph Moser. This book will help the client to understand that grieving isn't an illness, it's a natural process that every individual eventually has to experience. The book also brings practical methods of coping with grief. But most of all, the book allows the reader to understand that their grief will eventually pass and there will be better feelings once the grief passes. Their feelings of loss will never completely pass, but they will subside. (Moser).

Utilize the miracle question. The counselor and client will discuss how life would be ideal if the client were to wake up tomorrow and find things the way they wanted them to be. The counselor and client will list the ways the client sees their life as better and discuss ways that they can work toward those feelings to contentment.

LESSONS: BEGINNING TO TALK ABOUT THE LOSS

Story Telling:

Have the client repeat stories about the loved one to anyone that will listen. Make a list of those who may be willing to listen and discuss appropriate times to have such conversations. Ask the client to discuss memorable events involving the loved one.

Letter writing:

Have the client write a good-bye letter to the loved one and bring it to the next session. Encourage her to find a quiet place to write and to brainstorm using the following questions:

- What thoughts and feelings did you have soon after he/she died?
- What are some of the things you miss about him/her?
- Is there anything you wished you could have said or done before he/she died?
- Do you ever think that his/her death was your fault or that you could have prevented it?

- How has his/her death affected you?
- Is there anything that has happened since his/her death that you want to share with him/her?
- How did knowing him/her change your life?
- What do you plan to do with your life now that he/she is gone?

Remind him/her that the list of questions is just a guide. He/she may not wish to answer all of them and may wish to include others. Upon his/her return with the letter, discuss it with him/her and help him/her decide what to do with it. Calling it a "good-by letter" will help the client realize that the loved one is really gone.

Reviewing and Re-experiencing:

Have the client bring in various items that elicit positive (or negative) emotions about the loved one. These items could be pictures, collections, hobbies, or other mementos. Keep the following questions in past tense.

- When did he/she get this object?
- What makes it special?
- Was it a special occasion?
- Did the object provoke any special emotion?
- What feelings surface now in response to this object?
- What feelings were present when you first obtained this object?

These questions require the client to think about the loved one and recall the past, which is an acknowledgement that the loved one is no longer alive. The negative emotions should be recognized, but saved for later work. The big issue now is just realizing the loved one is gone.

Things Have Changed:

Have the client make a list of everyday occurrences as well as a few special occasions. Then I'd have him/her tell me how each is different now that the loved one is gone. This would bring into realization the fact that the loved one is in fact gone. Use the following format:

Occurrences/Special Occasions	How They Are Different

TO HELP ADOLESCENTS COPE

Aim: To help adolescents cope with a loss.

Methods: Write a eulogy to the person in your life whom you need to let go of in death. In the eulogy emphasize their positive contributions to others in their life and capture their goodness, zest for life, and energy. Once you have completed this task, you may recognize that the person wanted you to let go. If they had lived, they would never have been as productive and would have never enjoyed life as much as they once had.

Write your own eulogy if you are having problems considering your letting go of life when the time comes. By reviewing your own life, you may recognize the need to let go once its quality is diminished due to terminal or severely debilitating illness.

Write a will and the plans for your funeral service. This will remind you of your mortality and the need for you to keep your priorities in life clear.

Write a "twenty-years-from-now" autobiography of yourself, emphasizing the changes in your life then if you let go of:

1. guilt

2. grief

3. dependency

4. over-responsibility

5. resistance to change

6. fear

7. anger

8. denial

9. any other unhealthy behavior in your current life

   (http://www.coping.org/grief/letgo.htm.)

The therapist and client will discuss any information that the client got from the previous exercise and what it meant to her. The therapist and client will discuss how she is going to work through each problem and how the aspect of implementing the ritual will be affected.

PREPARE THE MOURNER FOR IMPLEMENTATION OF FUNERAL RITUALS

Aim: To prepare the mourner for the implementation of the ritual.

Method: The therapist will encourage the client to write a letter concerning her thoughts and feelings during this time.

Writing a Letter to a Deceased Loved One

Writing a letter is a powerful way to reconnect with a loved one after he or she has died. Here are some sample questions you might ask yourself as you write:

- What experiences have I been through since my loved one's death?
- What do I miss?
- What do I regret?
- What issues in our relationship remain unresolved?
- What do I appreciate?
- What have I learned about myself, my loved one, and my relationship?
- What do I want to carry on?

Ask yourself the following questions after you have written your letter:

- Was I open and honest?
- Did I express my love and appreciation
- Did I address unresolved issues in our relationship?
- Do I still feel regrets?
- Are any resentments still bothering me?
- Is anything left unsaid?
- Do I feel forgiveness? Do I feel more understanding?

(http://www.alexandrakennedy.com/index.html.)

Process the Ritual Experience

The therapist and client will discuss the ritual experience. We will discuss thoughts and feelings that occurred during the process and feelings that she is encountering now. How are they different? Did she make peace with the death through the ritual?

The therapist will monitor the client for any issues that develop regarding unfinished business and they will be discussed immediately.

CHAPTER 7

Apparent Competence

Apparent competence is the tendency for the individual to appear deceptively more competent than she actually is; usually due to failure of competencies to generalize across expected moods, situations, and time, and failure to display adequate nonverbal cues of emotional distress. Dialectical Behavior Therapy teaches other skills that will help children with emotional dysregulation. Linehan (1993) presented multiple activities to assist individuals in organizing themselves, in learning to attend to tasks, and in learning self-modulation.

DISTRACTION SKILLS: DISTRESS TOLERANCE (Linehan,1993b)

ACCEPTS with Modifications for Children and Adolescents

> **A**ctivities:
>
> **C**ontributing:
>
> **C**omparisons:
>
> **E**motions:
>
> **P**ushing away:
>
> **T**houghts:
>
> **S**ensations:

The "A" in ACCEPTS

Activities: Engage in exercise or hobbies; do cleaning; go to events; call or visit a friend; play computer games; go walking; work; play sports; go out to eat, have a decaf coffee or tea; go fishing; chop wood, do gardening; play pinball.

ACTIVITY CARD

This morning I will:

1. _____

2. _____

3. _____

4. _____

5. _____

This afternoon or evening I will:

1. _____

2. _____

3. _____

4. _____

5. _____

I must do this to keep from being overcome by my thoughts or problems.

The "C" in ACCEPTS

Contributing: Contribute to someone; do volunteer work; give something to someone else; make something nice for someone else; do a surprising, thoughtful thing.

To Contribute

This is what I can do to contribute and take my mind off myself:

1. _____

2. _____

3. _____

4. _____

5. _____

I, _____, promise that I will carry out these activities.

Date: _____

The Second "C" in ACCEPTS

Comparisons: Compare yourself to people coping the same as you or not as well as you. Compare yourself to those less fortunate than you. Watch soap operas. Read about disasters, others' suffering.

COMPARISON CARD

I know that I feel upset because _____, but I know that _____ has it a lot worse than I do. I also know that _____ manages to get through things so I can too. One way that I can manage to get through this is to _____.

The "E" in ACCEPTS

Emotions: Read emotional books or stories, old letters; go to emotional movies; listen to emotional music. Be sure the event creates different emotions. Ideas: scary movies, joke books, comedies, funny records, religious music, marching songs, "I Am Woman" (Helen Reddy); going to a store and reading funny greeting cards

For Youths

I agree to read: _____

whenever I feel sad or worried. I agree to watch _____ whenever I

feel sad or worried.

The "P" in ACCEPTS

Pushing away: Push the situation away by leaving it for a while. Leave the situation mentally. Build an imaginary wall between yourself and the situation. Push the situation away by blocking it in your mind. Censor ruminating. Refuse to think about the painful aspects of the situation. Put the pain on a shelf. Box it up and put it away for a while.

For Children and Adolescents

In your office, have the child construct a worry box. A recipe box that can be personally decorated or a small cardboard box that can be decorated will do. Have them write or draw the thought or memory that is bugging them. Then have the youth place the thought or memory in the box so that it can be left with you or a capable adult.

The "T" in ACCEPTS

Thoughts: Count to 10
Count colors in a painting or trees, windows
Work puzzles
Watch TV
Read

The "S" in ACCEPTS

Sensations: Hold ice in your hand
Squeeze a rubber ball very hard
Stand under a very hard and hot shower
Listen to very loud music
Put a rubber band on wrist, pull out, and let go

TO ATTEND TO SLEEP PROBLEMS:

Make sure that you understand the differences between insomnia and hypersomnia. Simply stated, insomnia is the inability to fall asleep or stay asleep, the tendency to awaken early in the morning, or the sense of light and non-refreshing sleep. If a teenager stays up all night or a child constantly wakes up at night, then insomnia may be the culprit. Sometimes proper adherence to sleep hygiene rules can be helpful in producing a more rapid resolution to this type of insomnia.

Sleep Hygiene

Examples of sleep hygiene measures include:
- Maintain a regular bedtime schedule
- Avoid excessive time in bed
- Avoid taking naps
- Use the bed only for sleeping
- Do not watch the clock
- Do something relaxing before bedtime
- Make the bedroom as quiet as possible
- Avoid the consumption of alcohol and caffeine within 2 hours of bedtime
- Exercise moderately, regularly, and not within 4 hours of bedtime
- Avoid going to bed hungry
- Learn strategies to make bedtime as relaxing and tension-free as possible

The Sleep Diary

Directions: For older children and teenagers, using a sleep diary will help you and the young person get a handle on how the young person handles (or does not handle) sleeping. You would tell the young person that the Sleep Diary is used to take inventory of sleeping patterns. Keep a sleep diary/journal for at least 2 weeks to help identify specific problems. The diary/journal should include: time you go to bed, how long it took to fall asleep, when you wake up, nap times, emotions you felt that day, amount and type of exercise, foods you ate/drank that day (especially note caffeine, alcohol, nicotine). A sleep diary will help identify patterns in sleep behaviors. The Sleep Diary looks like this:

Answer in the morning after waking for the day

	At what time did you first go to bed?	How long did it take you to fall asleep?	Overall, how many hours did you sleep?	At what time did you wake up (for the last time) this morning?	In general, how did you feel when you woke up? (Very refreshed, somewhat refreshed, fatigued)	On a scale of 1–5, how well did you sleep last night? (5=didn't wake; 1=woke 4x)
Day 1						
Day 2						
Day 3						
Day 4						
Day 5						
Day 6						
Day 7						

Answer at bedtime just before you go to sleep.

	How much time, if any, did you spend napping during the day?	Did you consume any of these substances during the day? **Caffiene** (within 6 hrs of bedtime) **Alcohol** (within 1 hr of bedtime) **Medication** Type: _____	On a scale of 1 to 5, how would you rate your overall mood and functioning during the day? **5** = positive and energetic **1** = depressed and lethargic	List all activities within two hours of bedtime.
Day 1				
Day 2				
Day 3				
Day 4				
Day 5				
Day 6				
Day 7				

After charting the sleep habits of the youth, discuss anything like naps, caffeine use, etc. that would interfere with sleeping and develop a plan to follow that will help the young person incorporate sleep hygiene habits. The plan would look like this:

I _____ will:
(client's name)

_____ Maintain a regular bedtime schedule.

_____ Avoid excessive time in bed.

_____ Avoid taking naps.

_____ Use the bed only for sleeping.

_____ Will not watch the clock.

_____ Do something relaxing before bedtime. This includes:

_____

_____

_____

_____ Make the bedroom as quiet as possible.

_____ Avoid the consumption of alcohol and caffeine within 2 hours of bedtime

_____ Exercise moderately, regularly, and not within 4 hours of bedtime.

_____ Avoid going to bed hungry.

Hypersomnia is characterized by recurrent episodes of excessive daytime sleepiness or prolonged nighttime sleep. People with hypersomnia are usually compelled to nap repeatedly during the day often at inappropriate times (school, conversation, meals). Hypersomnia usually affects adolescents and young adults. Treatment for hypersomnia includes: changes in behavior, diet, good sleep hygiene and sometimes medication such as: amphetamine, methylphenidate, modafinil, clonidine, levodopa, antidepressants all which require the intervention of a medical doctor.

Build a "life worth living" (Linehan, 1993b)

- Work toward goals: ACCUMULATE POSITIVES
- Make list of positive events you want
- List small steps toward goals
- Take first step

To Increase Positive Emotions

- ATTEND TO RELATIONSHIPS
- Repair old relationships
- Reach out for new relationships
- Work on current relationships

ATTENDING TO RELATIONSHIPS

Clients must learn to recognize, define, and refine how they wish to meet their relationship needs. They are asked to define what they want from their family, friends, work, school, and life. They are even asked to define what it is that they want from the counselor and themselves. Some questions asked are:

1. "If you were the person that you wished you could be, what kind of person would that be?" _____

    _____

    _____

2. "What would your family be like if your wants and their wants matched?"

    _____

    _____

3. "What would you be doing if you were living as you want to?"

    _____

    _____

4. "What is it that you don't seem to be getting from life?" _____

    _____

    _____

5. "What can you do to make the relationship with _____ better?"

    _____

    _____

    _____

Be mindful of positive experiences

FOCUS attention on positive events that happen.

REFOCUS when your mind wanders to the negative.

What If You Don't Know What Pleasant Activities Are?

Linehan (1993b) developed a list of such activities that she named the *Adult Pleasant Events Schedule*

For Young People

Go through the activity list below and mark approximately six activities for you to schedule into your weekly timetable.

Activity List

How to indulge yourself

_____ Do your hair

_____ Paint your nails

_____ Take a bubble bath

_____ Eat your favorite food

_____ Go shopping to buy yourself a little present

_____ Call your friends and plan a date

_____ Buy your favorite book or magazine

_____ Play your favorite computer game

_____ Color in your favorite coloring book

_____ Watch your favorite cartoon or TV show

Energetic activities

_____ Go for a walk

_____ Collect leaves

_____ Play a game

_____ Go for a swim

_____ Go for a bike ride

_____ Go fishing

_____ Take the dog for a walk

_____ Go jogging

_____ Kick a ball around

_____ Plant flowers

_____ Go rollerskating or rollerblading

_____ Lift weights

_____ Play your favorite sport

Activities out and about

_____ Go to a movie

_____ Go shopping

_____ Go out to dinner

_____ Visit the local zoo or theme park

_____ Go to the markets

_____ Go and borrow a book you are interested in from the local library

_____ Go to the art gallery or museum

_____ Watch a sports game you are interested in

_____ Go dancing

Household activities

_____ Do some room cleaning

_____ Do a little gardening

_____ Rearrange the furniture

_____ Organize something that has been bothering you

_____ Do some sewing

_____ Play with your dog or cat

_____ Choose something interesting or novel to cook

Private activities

_____ Listen to music

_____ Dance to some music

_____ Write a letter or email to a friend

_____ Play a computer game

_____ Read a good book, magazine or newspaper

_____ Play a solitary card game

_____ Teach yourself something new

Social activities

_____ Give a friend a call

_____ Meet a friend for coffee or dinner

_____ Go on a picnic with a friend

_____ Play with your friends

_____ Go out with some friends

Add your own examples

_____

_____

_____

Modulation Activities

So what we have just covered are multiple methods to overcome emotional dysregulation. These skills must be learned sometime in life to function appropriately in life and in school.

Cannot Tolerate Stress

The non-acceptance or oversimplification of the original problems precludes the type of attention, support, and diligent training such an individual needs. Thus, the child does not learn to adequately label or control emotional reactions. Second, by oversimplifying the ease of solving life's problems, the environment does not teach the child to tolerate distress or to form realistic goals and expectations (Linehan, 1993, p. 51).

Teaching Stress Tolerance

Teaching stress tolerance takes many forms. As counselors, we need to teach stress tolerance to children and adolescents.

Distress Tolerance Skills

In crises people are more interested in showing others how bad a situation is rather than surviving the situation. This is understandable when their crisis situations were invalidated when they were growing up. The problem with proving how bad things are is that it *hardly ever works.* Rather than listening to teens and kids rattle on about how bad life is, listen but then take control of session and teach distress tolerance skills.

Self-Soothing Skills

A way to remember these skills is to think of soothing each of your five senses.

    FIVE SENSES:
1. Vision
2. Hearing
3. Smell
4. Taste
5. Touch

With Vision:
- Buy one beautiful flower; make one space in a room pretty; light a candle and watch the flame.
- Set a pretty place at the table, using your best things, for a meal.
- Go to a museum with beautiful art. Go sit in the lobby of a beautiful old hotel.
- Look at nature around you.
- Go out in the middle of the night and watch the stars. Walk in a pretty part of town.
- Fix your nails so they look pretty. Look at beautiful pictures in a book.
- Go to a ballet or other dance performance, or watch one on TV.
- Be mindful of each sight that passes in front of you, not lingering on any.

With Hearing:
- Listen to beautiful or soothing music, or to invigorating and exciting music.
- Pay attention to sounds of nature (waves, birds, rainfall, leaves rustling).
- Sing to your favorite songs.
- Hum a soothing tune.
- Learn to play an instrument.
- Call a friend just to hear a human voice.
- Be mindful of any sounds that come your way, letting them go in one ear and out the other.

With Smell:
- Use your favorite perfume or lotions, or try them on in the store; spray fragrance in the air; light a scented candle.
- Put lemon oil on your furniture.
- Put potpourri in a bowl in your room.
- Boil cinnamon; bake cookies, cake, or bread.
- Smell the roses.
- Walk in a wooded area and mindfully breathe in the fresh smells of nature.

With Taste:
- Have a good meal; have a favorite soothing drink such as herbal tea or hot chocolate (no alcohol); treat yourself to a dessert.
- Put whipped cream on your coffee.
- Sample flavors in an ice cream store.
- Suck on a piece of peppermint candy.
- Chew your favorite gum.
- Get a little bit of a special food you don't usually spend the money on, such as fresh-squeezed orange juice.
- Really taste the food you eat; eat one thing mindfully.

With Touch:
- Take a bubble bath; put clean sheets on the bed. Pet your dog or cat.
- Have a massage; soak your feet.
- Put creamy lotion on your whole body.
- Put a cold compress on your forehead.
- Sink into a really comfortable chair in your home.
- Put on a silky blouse, dress, or scarf.
- Try on fur-lined gloves or fur coats in a department store.
- Brush your hair for a long time.
- Hug someone. Experience whatever you are touching; notice touch that is soothing.

Not Only Self-Soothe, Improve the Moment

Instead of giving in to a crisis, the child or teen can learn to "improve the moment" or focus in such a way that s/he begins to control self. A way to remember these skills is the word:

IMPROVE

The I in IMPROVE: Imagery

With Imagery:
- Imagine very relaxing scenes.
- Imagine a secret room within yourself, seeing how it is decorated.
- Go into the room whenever you feel very threatened.
- Close the door on anything that can hurt you.
- Imagine everything going well. Imagine coping well.
- Make up a fantasy world that is calming and beautiful and let your mind go with it.
- Imagine hurtful emotions draining out of you like water out of a pipe.

A SHORT GUIDELINE FOR TEACHING
Teaching Relaxation by Means of Guided Imagery

Place the client in a quiet, calm environment that is free from other distractions such as noise, strong light, or extraneous conversation. You might choose to sit away from the direct gaze of the person and ask him or her to select a place that has been conducive to rest and peace in the past. Then, ask the client to close his or her eyes, if desired, and to imagine that peaceful place. Ask the client to describe the place in terms of its appearances its odors if appropriate, and other sensual characteristics such as its temperature. Use a quiet, subdued tone of voice to avoid interrupting the mood that is being established. Should the client identify a place such as the beach, you can prompt responses with such non-threatening questions as "What does the sky look like? 'What color is it? Is the air warm? How does the warm sand feel to your body? Are you alone on the beach?" You also could say "Tell me how the water feels to your foot. Tell me more about the things that you think and do at the beach." All of these questions require that the client focus on the place that is being described. Gradually, his or her focus on the stressful event is weakened, resulting in a temporary diminution of anxiety. Relaxation occurs as a result of associations with the non-threatening and calming beach.

The M in IMPROVE: Meaning

With **Meaning:**

- Find or create some purpose, meaning, or value in the pain.
- Remember, listen to, or read about spiritual values.
- Focus on whatever positive aspects of a painful situation you can find.
- Repeat them over and over in your mind.
- Make lemonade out of lemons.
- Set some goals for yourself.

SETTING GOALS

Directions: Tell the client the following facts:

- We all need goals to work towards

- We have no way of evaluating if we are getting somewhere unless we can see if we have made it to our goals.

- It is important to set small goals. If the goals are too overwhelming, it will do more harm than good.

- Goals only assist us if they are flexible and re-evaluated as time passes. If the goals are rigid, then they can do more harm than good.

Area	Short Term (Next Week)	Mid Term (Next Month)	Long Term (Next Year)
Recreational Activitites			
Family Life			
Health			
Relationships			
Personal Development			
School			

Once you have set yourself some goals, it is easier to try and work out what the intervening steps would be to get there.

Remember, as time goes on, you may need to stop and re-evaluate your goals.

The P in IMPROVE: Prayer

With **Prayer:**
- Open your heart to a supreme being, greater wisdom, God, your own wise mind.
- Ask for strength to bear the pain in this moment.
- Turn things over to God or a higher being.

The R in IMPROVE: Relaxation

With **Relaxation:**
- Try muscle relaxing by tensing and relaxing each large muscle group, starting with your hands and arms, going to the top of your head, and then working down
- Listen to a relaxation tape
- Exercise hard
- Take a hot bath or sit in a hot tub
- Drink hot milk
- Massage your neck and scalp, your calves and feet.
- Get in a tub filled with very cold or hot water and stay in it until the water is tepid.
- Breathe deeply; half-smile; change facial expression.

The O in IMPROVE: One Thing

With **One Thing** in the moment:
- Focus your entire attention on just what you are doing right now.
- Keep yourself in the very moment you are in; put your mind in the present.
- Focus your entire attention on physical sensations that accompany non-mental tasks (e.g. walking, washing, doing dishes, cleaning, fixing).
- Be aware of how your body moves during each task.
- Do awareness exercises.

The V in IMPROVE: Vacation

With a brief **Vacation:**
- Give yourself a brief vacation.
- Get in bed and pull the covers up over your head for 20 minutes.
- Ask your roommate to bring you coffee in bed or make you dinner (offer to reciprocate).
- Make yourself milk toast, bundle up in a chair, and eat it slowly.
- Take a blanket to the park and sit on it for a whole afternoon.
- Unplug your phone for a day, or let your answering machine screen your calls.
- Take a 1-hour breather from hard work that must be done.

The E in IMPROVE: Encouragement

With **Encouragement:**
- Be a cheerleader for yourself. Repeat over and over: "I can stand it."
- "It won't last forever"
- "I will make it out of this"
- "I'm doing the best I can do."

AFFIRMATION COLLAGE

Directions: An affirmation collage is a tool we use to visualize how we see ourselves and the manner in which we experience our lives. You will develop an affirmation collage that will be a picture of how you see yourself right now. It can contain pictures, words, or symbols that are a reflection of those qualities that express you. Then we will make a second collage showing how you wish you were, showing the qualities you want to attain, and the goals you want to achieve in your life. We will cut out pictures and word symbols from magazines, catalogs, newspapers, and old books and glue them together so that you can show me how you see your life right now and how you would like to see your life.

Select one page to represent how you see yourself right now and another page to represent yourself the way you would like to be. Choose appropriate pictures to express the particular feeling, quality, goal, or material item you want to share. Let your imagination soar. Glue the pictures to the pages.

Now, let's look at the pictures and you explain the differences in yourself now and how you would like to be in the future. We will use this chart:

The Way I Am   **The Way I Would Like to Be**

One at a time, let's take the way you are and have you tell me what steps you could take to become the way you would like to be:

1. I am _____

_____

In order to change I must:

a. _____

b. _____

c. _____

2. I am _____

_____

In order to change I must:

a. _____

b. _____

c. _____

3. I am _____

_____

In order to change I must:

a. _____

b. _____

c. _____

4. I am _____

_____

In order to change I must:

a. _____

b. _____

c. _____

5. I am _____

_____

In order to change I must:

a. _____

b. _____

c. _____

6. I am _____

_____

In order to change I must:

a. _____

b. _____

c. _____

7. I am _____

_____

In order to change I must:

a. _____

b. _____

c. _____

8. I am _____

_____

In order to change I must:

a. _____

b. _____

c. _____

9. I am _____

_____

In order to change I must:

a. _____

b. _____

c. _____

10. I am _____

_____

In order to change I must:

a. _____

b. _____

c. _____

Now out of these ten things you want to change, choose the one you will work on and sign this page showing me that you intend to change this one thing by next week.

I, _____, will work on change item number _____.
    (Client's signature)   *(Item #)*

SONG AFFIRMATION

Directions: This is just like the Affirmation Collage, but instead of giving the client paper and magazines to allow them self-expression, you hand them a tape recorder and tell them to record songs that will show you who they are right now. When they have the selection of songs, they will fill out the following form and bring both the form and the music back to you. In a session, you have them play the song and talk to you about their comments about themselves.

Title of Song: _____

What it says about me: _____

_____

Title of Song: _____

What it says about me: _____

_____

Title of Song: _____

What it says about me: _____

_____

Then have the client choose and record songs explaining how they would like to be. When they have the selection of songs, they will fill out the following form and bring both the form and the music back to you. In a session, you have them play the song and talk to you about their comments about themselves.

Title of Song: _____

What it tells you about the way I would like to be: _____

_____

Title of Song: _____

What it tells you about the way I would like to be: _____

_____

Title of Song: _____

What it tells you about the way I would like to be: _____

_____

One at a time, let's take the way you are and have you tell me what steps you could take to become the way you would like to be:

1. I am _____

_____

In order to change I must:

a. _____

b. _____

c. _____

2. I am _____

_____

In order to change I must:

a. _____

b. _____

c. _____

3. I am _____

_____

In order to change I must:

a. _____

b. _____

c. _____

4. I am _____

_____

In order to change I must:

a. _____

b. _____

c. _____

5. I am _____

_____

In order to change I must:

a. _____

b. _____

c. _____

Now out of these five things you want to change, choose the one you will work on and sign this page showing me that you intend to change this one thing by next week.

I, _____, will work on change item number _____.
(Client's signature)   *(Item #)*

TECHNIQUES FOR CHILDREN: HANDLING WORRIES

Children with anxiety benefit from learning to reduce both physical stress and worrying thoughts. With these activities it is important to tailor the details to suit the needs of the child to maximize impact. These activities can run alongside many other therapy aims and they can also help prepare the child for more intensive work that mayneed to be done.

WORRY BOX: AGE 5 TO 12 YEARS

Aim: To reduce fears and anxieties by helping the child to learn to set them aside.

Materials: A little box which the child can keep. A set of blank cards (approximately twelve, small enough to fit into the box) or slips of paper.

Method: Talk to the child about how we all have worries and that puffing them away can help to get rid of them so that we can get on with life. Ask the child to decorate the box in a manner which she sees fit, and talk about where the box of worries can live. The box needs to be some distance away from the child to illustrate the point that she does not have to carry her worries with her. For example, they could be deep in a cupboard or in another room. If the child is worrying about matters that adults should be concerned about (for example, if her little brother is naughty), it is appropriate to give the box each day to the caregiver when it completed. This will illustrate to the child that it is the adults should be carrying that responsibility.

Next, take the set of cards and ask the child about the worry she would like to put away. Write each worry down on a separate card or piece of paper. Then, ritually, have the child put the worry in the box, giving positive reasons why she need not be concerned about them. Now put the lid down. The child may like to seal box with some tape or a ribbon. Finally, put the box away together in the place already discussed, or give it to the caregiver if the place is at home. The adult caregiver then has the responsibility ensuring the box is put in the place the child has chosen.

Some children like to leave the box with the therapist. This can be useful if you plan to work on the worries with the child in the next session.

Variation: *Free to Sleep*. With sleepless children whose problem is caused by worrying, the caregiver may wish to use the box each night. The caregiver discusses the child's worries with her; they are written on cards, put in the box and, after reassuring the child about each worry, the caregiver takes them away. As the caregiver removes the box he asks the child to think of three good things to talk about in the morning.

Besides improving, list PROS and CONS:

Sometimes children and adolescents would rather be upset than handle stress and other problems. You don't want them to give into stress and create crises. Another stress tolerance skill involves sitting down and making a list of the pros and cons to giving in to a situation and turning it into a crisis.

Thinking of PROS AND CONS:

Make a list of the pros and cons of *tolerating* the distress. Make another list of the pros and cons of *not tolerating* the distress—that is, of coping by hurting yourself, abusing alcohol or drugs, or doing something else impulsive. Focus on long-term goals, the light at the end of the tunnel. Remember times when pain has ended. Think of the positive consequences of tolerating the distress. Imagine in your mind how good you will feel if you achieve your goals, if you don't act impulsively. Think of all of the negative consequences of not tolerating your current distress. Remember what has happened in the past when you have acted impulsively to escape the moment.

PROS AND CONS DECISION-MAKING METHOD

Directions: <u>Explain.</u> A simple process for decision-making is a pros and cons list.

Some decisions are a simple matter of whether to make a change or not, such as moving, taking a new job, or buying something, selling something, replacing something, etc. Other decisions involve number of options, and are concerned more with how to do something, involving a number of choices.

Steps:
1. First you will need a separate sheet of paper for each identified option.
2. On each sheet write clearly the option concerned, and then beneath it the headings 'pros' and 'cons' (or 'advantages' and 'disadvantages', or simply 'for' and 'against'). Many decisions simply involve the choice of whether to go ahead or not, to change or not; in these cases you need only one sheet.
3. Then write down as many effects and implications of the particular option that you (and others if appropriate) can think of, placing each in the relevant column.
4. If helpful 'weight' each factor, by giving it a score out of three or five points (eg., 5 being extremely significant, and 1 being of minor significance).
5. When you have listed all the points you can think of for the option concerned compare the number or total score of the items/effects/factors between the two columns.
6. This will provide a reflection and indication as to the overall attractiveness and benefit of the option concerned. If you have scored each

item you will actually be able to arrive at a total score, being the difference between the pros and cons column totals. The bigger the difference between the total pros and total cons then the more attractive the option is.

7. If you have a number of options and have complete a pros and cons sheet for each option, compare the attractiveness—points difference between pros and cons—for each option. The biggest positive difference between pros and cons is the most attractive option.

8. If you don't like the answer that the decision-making sheet(s) reflect back to you, it means you haven't included all the cons—especially the emotional ones, or you haven't scored the factors consistently, so revisit the sheet(s) concerned.

You will find that writing things down in this way will help you to see things more clearly, become more objective and detached, which will help you to make clearer decisions.

Below is an example of a pros and cons weighted decision-making sheet

---

Decision Option: Should I dare take Senior English?

<u>**Pros**</u>	<u>**Cons**</u>
Help me get into college (5)	Too much homework (5)
Have my favorite teacher (3)	Want to work (3)
Lots of my friends in the class (4)	Time and hassle (2)
Write better papers (3)	Big decisions scare me (4)
Sit next to Judy (3)	Big decisions like this scare and
It'll be a load off my mind (2)	upset me
Total 6 pros, total score 20	**Total 4 cons, total score 14**

On the basis of the pros and cons, and the weighting applied, in the above example there's a clear overall quantifiable benefit attached to the decision to go ahead and take Senior English. Notice that it's even possible to include 'intangible' emotional issues in the pros and cons comparison, for example 'it'll be a load off my mind', and 'decisions scare and upset me'. A decision-making pros and cons list like this helps remove the emotion which blocks clear thinking and decision-making—you can now see the wood

HELP WITH SETTING GOALS WITH TEENS

Goal-Setting Worksheet

The Process:

1. Identify a concern or a problem.

2. State the desired outcome of the problem.

3. Assess the desired outcome.

    a. Does it specify what you want to do?

4. In what ways is achievement of this goal important to you? To others?

5. What will achieving the goal require of you? Of others?

6. To what extent is this goal something you want to do?

7. Is this goal based on

    a. Logical ideas?

    b. Realistic expectations?

    c. Irrational ideas or thoughts?

    d. Perfectionistic standards?

8. How will achieving this goal help you?

9. What problems could achieving this goal create for you?

10. If this goal requires others to change, can you understand that such a change is not likely to occur and that you can only work on yourself?

11. Specify exactly what you will be

    a. Doing _____

    b. Thinking _____

    c. Feeling _____

12. Specify your goal definition by indicating:

    a. Where this will occur?

    b. When this will happen?

    c. With whom this will occur?

    d. How often this will happen?

13. Develop a plan that specifies *how you* will attain your goal by identifying action steps included in the plan.

    a. _____

    b. _____

    c. _____

    d. _____

    e. _____

14. Check your list of action steps:

    a. Are the gaps between steps small? If not, add a step or two.

    b. Does each step represent only one major activity? If not, separate this one step into two or more steps.

    c. Does each step specify what, where, when, with whom, and how much or how often? If not, go back and define your action steps more concretely.

15. Develop a goal pyramid to sequence your list of action steps, starting with the easiest, most immediate step on the top and proceeding to the bottom of the pyramid by degree of difficulty and immediacy or proximity to the goal.

16. For each action step (starting with the first), brainstorm what could make it difficult to carry out or could interfere with doing it successfully. Consider feelings, thoughts, places, people, and lack of knowledge or skills. Write down the obstacles.

17. For each action step (starting with the first), identify existing resources such as feelings, thoughts, situations, people and support systems, information, skills, beliefs, and self-confidence that would make it more likely for you to carry out the action or complete it more successfully. Write down the resources in the space provided.

18. Identify a way to monitor your progress for completion of each action step.

19. Develop a plan to help yourself maintain the action steps once you have attained them.

STEPS FOR THE COUNSELOR AND QUESTIONS THE COUNSELOR SHOULD ASK

1. **Explain the purpose and importance of having goals or positive out-comes to the client.**

    "Let's talk about some areas you would like to work on during counseling. This will help us to do things that are related to what you want to accomplish."

2. **Determine *positive* changes desired by client ("I would like" versus "can't").**

   "What would you like to be doing [thinking, feeling] differently?"

   "Suppose some distant relative you haven't seen for a while comes here in several months. What would be different then from the way things are now?"

   "Assuming we are successful, what do you want to be doing, or how would this change for you?"

   "In what ways do you want to benefit from counseling?"

3. **Determine whether the goal selected represents changes owned by the client rather than someone else ("I want to talk to my mom without yelling at her," rather than "I want my mom to stop yelling at me").**

   "How much control do you have to make this happen?"

   "What changes will this require of you?" "What changes will this require someone else to make?"

   "Can this be achieved without the help of anyone else?"

   "To whom is this change most important?"

4. **Identify advantages (positive consequences) to client and others of goal achievement.**

   "In what ways is it worthwhile to you and others to achieve this?"

   "How will achieving this goal help you?" "What problems will continue for you if you don't pursue this goal?"

   "What are the advantages of achieving this change—for you? others?"

   "Who will benefit from this change—and how?"

5. **Identify disadvantages (negative consequences) of goal achievement to client and others.**

   "What new problems in living might achieving this goal pose for you?"

   "Are there any disadvantages to going in this direction?"

   "How will achieving this change affect your life in adverse ways?"

   "How might this change limit or constrain you?"

6. **Identify whether, as the helper, you can pursue counseling with this particular client.**

   "These are things I am able to help you work with."

"I feel uncomfortable working with you on this issue because of my own personal values [or lack of knowledge]. I'd like to give you the names of several other counselors."

"This would be hard for me to help you with because it seems as if you're choosing something that will restrict you and not give you any options. Let's talk more about this."

7. **Identify what the client will be doing, thinking, or feeling in a concrete, observable way as a result of goal achievement ("I want to be able to talk to my mom without yelling at her," rather than "I want to get along with my mom").**

   "What do you want to be able to do [think, feel] differently?"

   "What would I see you doing [thinking, feeling] after this change?"

   "Describe a good and a poor example of this goal."

8. **Specify under what conditions and what situations goals will be achieved: When, where, and with whom ("I want to be able to talk to my mom at home during the next month without yelling at her").**

   "When do you want to accomplish this goal?"

   "Where do you want to do this?" "With whom?"

   "In what situations?"

9. **Specify how often or how much a client will do something to achieve goal ("I want to be able to talk to my mom at home during the next month without yelling at her at least once a day").**

   "How much [or how often] are you doing this [or feeling this way] now?" "What is a realistic increase or decrease?" "How much [or how often] do you want to be doing this to be successful at your goal?"

   "What amount of change is realistic, considering where you are right now?"

10. **Identify and list small action steps the client will need to take to reach the goal (that is, break the big goal down into little subgoals).**

    "How will you go about doing [thinking, feeling] this?"

    "What exactly do you need to do to make this happen?"

    "Let's brainstorm some actions you'll need to take to make your goal work for you."

    "What have you done in the past to work toward this goal?"

    "How did it help?"

    "Let's think of the steps you need to take to get from where you are now to where you want to be."

List of Action Steps

1.

2.

3.

4.

5.

6.

7.

8.

9.

10.

11. **Sequence the action steps on the goal pyramid (a hierarchy) in terms of**

    a. degree of difficulty (least to most)

    b. immediacy (most to least immediate)

    "What is your first step? What would you be able to do most easily?"

    "What would be most difficult? What is your foremost priority? What is most important for you to do soon? least important?"

    "How could we order these steps to maximize your success in reaching your goal?"

    "Let's think of the steps you need to take to get from where you are now to where you want to be and arrange them in an order from what seems easiest to you to the ones that seem hardest."

    "Can you think of some things you need to do before some other things as you make progress toward this outcome?"

12. **Identify any people, feelings, or situations that could prevent the client from taking action to reach the goal.**

    "What are some obstacles you may encounter in trying to take this action?"

    "What people [feelings, ideas, situations] might get in the way of getting this done?"

"In what ways could you have difficulty completing this task successfully?"

"What do you need to know to take this action?" or *"What skills do you need to have?"*

13. **Identify any resources (skill, knowledge, support) that the client needs to take into action to meet the goal.**

   "What resources do you have available to help you as you complete this activity?"

   "What particular thoughts or feelings are you aware of that might make it easier for you to _____."

   "What kind of support system do you have from others that you can use to make it easier to _____."

   "What skills [or information] do you possess that will help you do this successfully?"

14. **Develop a plan to evaluate progress toward the goal.**

   "Would it be practical for you to rate these feelings [count the times you do this] during the next two weeks? This information will help us determine the progress you are making."

   "Let's discuss a way you can keep track of how easy or hard it is for you to take these steps this week."

Short-term Plans

   • Can be accomplished immediately
   • Get you something small you want here and now
   • May or may not result in long-term need satisfaction

Long-term Plans

   • You may have to forego short-term plans
   • May be difficult to sustain
   • Result in greater meaning over the long haul

QUESTIONS TO ASK

   What is going to prompt or remind you to actually do these things?

   What are the obstacles or barriers to accomplishing your plans?

   What has made it difficult for you to do these things in the past?

   What, if anything, do you stand to lose by engaging in these plans?

How much of what you need to accomplish these plans relies on others' efforts?

If you're relying on others, what do you have to offer them that can make them more likely to want to assist you?

Are you trying to do too much?

Are you trying to do too little?

Make reasonable, sustainable goals.

Can you lower your short-term expectations in service of your long-term wants and needs?

How much is your sense of urgency interfering with your accomplishment of your goals?

How is your behavior being influenced by your moods?

Exercise: Write your Short- and Long-Term Goals & Plans

Goal: _____

Short Term Plans	**Long Term Plans**
_____	_____
_____	_____
_____	_____
_____	_____

Watch for Mood-Dependent Behavior

- You do the behavior because of the mood you're in
- More an expression of mood than a goal or purpose
- "Killing the messenger" is an example
- Not strategic or wise

Use Strategic Behavior

- Be aware of your mood in you're in when responding to situations important to you
- Is this behavior what will really get me what I want?

Break It Down

- What is the environmental (external) prompt?
- What is happening to which you are about to respond?
- What is your mood?

- What is your short-term goal or objective?
- What is your long-term goal or objective?
- What behavior (action) will accomplish your goal?

Compare to Results

- If you express your mood in this moment, will it interfere with your long-term or short-term objectives?
- Will it interfere or enhance your goal obtainment?

With High Emotions, We Forget

- Mood-dependent behavior is not strategic
- Mood-dependent behavior is not wise

Use A Problem-Solving, Strategic Approach to Life

Homework

Write a list of mood-dependent behaviors you know you have at least occasionally engaged in. Write how it helped or hurt both your long-term and short-term goal objectives.

Mood-dependent Behavior	Helped or Hurt Short-term goals	Helped or Hurt Long-term goals

REFERENCES AND RESOURCES

All Feelings Are Okay—It's What You Do With Them That Counts. Retrieved on March 3, 2007 from www.guidancechannel.com.

Beck, A. T. (1976). *Cognitive therapy and the emotional disorders.* New York: International Universities Press.

Bisignano, J. & McElmurry, M. (1987). *The changing years: My journal of personal growth.* Carthage, IL: Good Apple, Inc.

Callahan, C. (2008). Threat assessment in school violence. In T. Miller (Ed.) *School violence and primary prevention.* (pp. 59–77). New York: Springer Publishing.

Linehan, M. (1993a). *Cognitive-behavioral treatment of borderline personality disorder.* New York: Guilford Press.

Linehan, M. (1993b). *Skills training manual for treating borderline personality disorder.* New York: Guilford Press.

Linehan, M. (1995). CD: *Treating borderline personality disorder: The dialectal approach.* New York: Guilford Publication.

"Face It!" Retrieved on March 3, 2007 from www.guidancechannel.com.

Freud, S., (1913). *Totem and taboo.* London: Hogarth Press.

Goldman, L. (2004). Counseling with children in contemporary society. *Journal of Mental Health Counseling, 26,* 129–135.

Goldfried, M.R., & Davison, G.C. (1976). *Clinical behavior therapy.* New York: Holt, Rinehart & Winston.

Gotlib, I. H., & Krasnoperova, E. (1998). Biased information processing as a vulnerability factor for depression. *Behavior Therapy, 29,* 603–617.

Moser, Adolph. *Don't Despair on Thursday.* Retrieved on March 3, 2007 from www.guidancechannel.com.

O'Neill, R., Horner, R., Albin, R., Sprague, J., Storey, K., and Newton, J. (2006). *Functional assessment and program development for problem behavior.* New York: Brooks/Cole.

Padesky, C. A. (1996, February). *When there isn't enough time: Cognitive therapy innovations.* Clinical workshop, San Francisco, CA.

Rado, S. (1956). *Psychoanalysis of behavior: Collected papers.* New York: Grune & Stratton.

Rando, T. (1984). *Grief, dying, and death: Clinical interventions for caregivers.* Champaign, IL: Research Press.

Riethmayer, J. (1993). *About life & loss.* Bryan, TX: BJR Enterprises.

Schmideberg, M. (1947). The treatment of psychopaths and borderline patients. *American Journal of Psychotherapy, 1,* 49–55.

Segal, Z. V. (1988). Appraisal of the self-schema construct in cognitive models of depression. *Psychological Bulletin, 103,* 147–162.

Sometimes You Have to Say Goodbye. Retrieved on March 3, 2007 from www.guidancechannel.com.

"The Goodbye Game" Retrieved on March 3, 2007 from www.guidancechannel.com.

Williams, J. M. G. (1992). Autobiographical memory and emotional disorders. In S. A. Christianson (Ed.), *The handbook of emotion and memory* (pp. 451–476). Hillsdale, NJ: Erlbaum.

DBT Texts for Professionals

Linehan, M. M. (1993a). *Cognitive-behavioral treatment of borderline personality disorder.* New York: Guilford Press.

Linehan, M. (1993b). *Skills training manual for treating borderline personality disorder.* New York: Guilford Press.

Linehan, M. (1996). Dialectcal behavior therapy for borderline personality disorder. In B. Schmitz (Ed.), *Treatment of personality disorders* (pp. 179–199). Munich, Germany: Psychologie Verlags Union.

Marra, T. (2005). *Dialectal behavior therapy in private practice: A practical and comprehensive guide.* Oakland: New Harbinger Press.

Texts for Professionals

Germer, C, Siegal, R., & Fulton, P. Eds. (2005). *Mindfulness and psychotherapy.* New York: Guilford.

Hayes, S., Strosahl, K., Follette, V., & Linehan, M., Eds. (2004). *Mindfulness and acceptance: Expanding the cognitive-behavioral tradition.* New York: Guilford

Hayes, S., Strosahl, K., & Houts,A. Eds. (1999). *A practical guide to acceptance and commitment therapy.* Springer: New York.

Hanh, T. (1976). *The miracle of mindfulness.* Boston: Beacon Press.

Hanh, T. (1992). *Peace in every step.* New York: Bantam.

Kabat-Zinn, J. (1990). *Full catastrophe living: Using the wisdom of your body and mind to face stress, pain, and illness.* New York: Dell

Kabat-Zinn, J. (1994). *Where you go there you are: mindfulness mediations in everyday living.* New York: Hyperion.

Marra, T. (2004). *Depressed and anxious: The dialectical behavior therapy workbook for overcoming depression and anxiety.* Oakland: New Harbinger Press.

Najavits, L. (2002). *Seeking safety: A treatment manual for PTSD and substance abuse.* New York: Guilford Publications.

Spradlin, S. (2003). *Don't let emotions run your life: How dialectical behavior therapy can put you in control.* Oakland: New Harbinger Press.

Made in the USA
San Bernardino, CA
27 November 2017